THE
Machiavellian
MANAGER'S
HANDBOOK
FOR SUCCESS

THE
Machiavellian
MANAGER'S HANDBOOK FOR SUCCESS

L. F. Gunlicks

The Libey Business Library

LIBEY PUBLISHING
INCORPORATED
A Regnery Gateway Subsidary

Washington, D.C.

Library of Congress Cataloging-In-Publication Data

Gunlicks, Lynn F., 1943–
The Machiavellian manager's handbook for success / Lynn F. Gunlicks.
p. cm.
ISBN 0-89526-510-9
1. Office politics. I. Title.
HF5386.5.G86 1992
658.4'095—dc20   92-17451
CIP

Published in the United States by
Libey Publishing Incorporated
A Regnery Gateway Subsidiary
1130 17th Street, NW
Washington, DC 20036

Distributed to the trade by
National Book Network
4720-A Boston Way
Lanham, MD 20706

Printed on acid free paper

Manufactured in the United States of America

2 4 6 8 10 9 7 5 3 1

To all the past, present, and future victims
of the Machiavellian Manager

ACKNOWLEDGMENTS

Foremost, I acknowledge all the Machiavellian Managers with whom I have worked, for they have provided me with most of the examples used in this handbook. And gladly do I acknowledge Jud Sage, friend, neighbor, author, and teacher, who rendered valuable assistance in the preparation of my manuscript as well as much needed encouragement.

CONTENTS

Contents

Part III
ENTERING INTO COMBAT WITH THE MACHIAVELLIAN MANAGER
OR
ESCAPING WITH YOUR SKIN

PREFACE

THE MACHIAVELLIAN MANAGER is everywhere: private corporations, small businesses, government agencies at all levels—federal, state, county, and municipal. He is found in the military and in quasi-governmental organizations. He is omnipresent, at every level of these organizations.

In accordance with Darwin's theory of the survival of the fittest, the Machiavellian Manager not only survives but thrives in most organizations today. This is possible because those organizations lack awareness of his strategies and techniques, and because otherwise responsible people in those firms are fond of his managerial style, even as they are blissfully unaware of the dangerous consequences he presents to their individual job security or the organization's productivity.

The Machiavellian Manager lives by one code: Whatever I can get by with to enhance my own career is acceptable. He defines success as the personal accumulation of power, prestige, and wealth. He is amoral. Everyone with whom he comes in contact is immediately assessed for his or her potential for enhancing his career. Only those who possess that potential have any value to him.

The Machiavellian Manager is usually outgoing, articulate, energetic, and visible, but not easily recognizable as a Machiavellian Manager. In fact, he labors at appearing to his superiors as just the opposite of what he really is. He appears to be charming, very polite, extremely cooperative, always on top of things, and intelligent—but not too intelligent—to those he can use. To those who cannot contribute to his career goals he is cool and superficially polite. And he is dangerous and utterly ruthless with anyone who impedes his way or openly opposes him.

Eventually, the Machiavellian Manager is very successful, and his career is usually marked by rapid advancement. Along his road to success, however, the landscape is strewn with bloodied bodies, like the aftermath of an airborne strafing attack. Amid the litter are ruined careers, former associates and colleagues reeling under psychological and physiological stress symptoms, broken families, and even suicides.

The Machiavellian Manager is a one-man disaster zone who may not even be recognizable as such until his damage is long since done.

This book is based on personal observations of

successful Machiavellian Managers, and not on scientific surveys or studies. A scientific approach would be useless. The Machiavellian Manager, the focus of this handbook, would never admit to the tactics he has so successfully utilized, tactics outlined herein. To reveal such tactics would violate his very principles.

The best way for you, the reader, to substantiate the authenticity of this book is either through confirmation based on your own experience or through speaking with some of the legions of people who have witnessed, or been victims of, the cunning of the Machiavellian Manager.

You can use this handbook in many ways, ranging from an entertainment source to a guidebook for study so as to apply its rules. Some of you may wish to be able to identify the Machiavellian Manager to avoid the carnage he eventually causes. Others of you, much to your dismay, now work for or with a Machiavellian Manager and urgently need to know how at least to survive, if not to win, your desperate struggle. Still others of you as high-level executives and managers need this handbook to help you identify, and weed out, Machiavellian Managers within your organizations, thereby perhaps ensuring that the Machiavellian Manager never has an opportunity to survive or succeed in your workplace. Finally, I hope this handbook will move all of us to reexamine our organizational behavior, and inspire some soul-searching.

Do not be fooled when you read parts I and II of this handbook. I am not advocating Machiavellian behaviors—I detest and deplore them. However, if we are to ever successfully enter into combat with Machiavellian Managers or escape with our skins, we must enter their minds and understand how they think.

Should any of you find this handbook offensive, immoral, tasteless, or unrealistic, I have only to say that you are prime potential victims of the Machiavellian Manager.

INTRODUCTION

NICCOLÒ MACHIAVELLI (1469–1527) was writing for princes in the traditional sense: chaps with castles, scepters, courts, crowns, and kingdoms. Under the definition then used, princes also included kings and emperors.

Early in American history our princes were politicians. We call them the Founding Fathers—Franklin, Jefferson, Washington, Madison, Hamilton, Adams, and the others. Their position in society was much like that of European royalty, without all the trimmings. Many early Americans even wanted the trimmings: a serious movement was afoot after the American Revolution to make George Washington King George I of America. The idea foundered on one pretty tough question: Who's next? George had no sons.

Since the latter decades of the nineteenth century, most of America's princes have been in business or other public areas rather than in government. Occasionally a prince will arise from the political ranks—John Kennedy is a prime example—but in fact most politicians are frogs. Would you like to kiss Jesse Helms? Or Teddy Kennedy? (In America, the status of prince is not automatically bestowed on every member of a family. Then again, if you look at the history of Europe's royal families you'll soon discover that many real princes were actually frogs.)

Anyway, America recognized what I have just said by calling our late nineteenth-century captains of industry "robber barons." Now a baron isn't a prince, but he's better than a frog. As to the robber part, well, that's what this book is about.

I conclude, therefore, with regard to being feared and loved, that men love at their own free will, but fear at the will of the prince, and that a wise prince must rely on what is in his power and not on what is in the power of others, and must only contrive to avoid incurring hatred. . . .

Machiavelli,
The Prince
1532

Part 1

BECOMING A PRINCE: ORGANIZATIONAL PLACEMENT STRATEGY

1

CHOOSING AN ORGANIZATIONAL VICTIM

If, then, one considers the procedure of the duke, it will be seen how firm were the foundations he had laid to his future power. . . .

YOU ARE BEGINNING your career as a Machiavellian Manager. The first thing to remember is that the rules in this handbook will work very effectively, no matter what private or government organization you choose in which to begin your career. However, if you select the right organization, you can speed up the time frames for your career advancement.

Following are some basic rules that should serve to get you into a position where you can become truly Machiavellian:

† Never choose an organization struggling for its existence. Employment in such an organization will mean only hard work and little time for you to apply the rules in this handbook. Let others less worthy than yourself seek the slow path of advancement through hard work.

† Beware of big-company names or prestigious organizations. These companies and government agencies often use their prestige and status to obstruct the career ladders of employees or to minimize rapid promotional opportunities. In addition, competition can be keen in such organizations.

† Search out relatively new companies or government agencies. These are in a building and expansion mode. In this regard there are two things to remember:

    a. Managers in these organizations may not have had time to establish firm power bases, thus making them vulnerable;

    b. New management positions will be created.

† Seek a company that has just landed a big contract, or a government agency that has just had a sizable budget increase. (The latter may be hard to find in times of fiscal austerity, but true Machiavellian Managers know that even in

the worst of times there are those who pros-
per.) Managers may be well entrenched in these
organizations, but their need to expand will create numerous opportunities you can exploit for
your own advancement.

† Never worry about cost-of-living factors.
By following the rules in this handbook, you will
advance rapidly and will have more than enough
money to address high cost-of-living expenses
no matter where the organization in which you
land is located.

† If you have a technical or scientific education, it can work to your advantage. Organizations whose products are scientific and technical
are prime targets for you. Employees in such
firms take great pride in their achievements, and
are usually less concerned about internal politics
and advancement into managerial positions. It
hardly needs mentioning that even if you lack a
scientific education, those organizations may
nevertheless be fruitful areas of investigation,
although you may have to invest a modest
amount of time learning some scientific jargon (a
simple task for a Machiavellian, who is by nature
an excellent imitator).

† Check out the ages of the managers of the
organizations you are considering. Those firms
where the majority of the managers are aging

will provide you with increased promotional opportunities. Some organizations will try to impress you with the fact that they have many young managers on their staffs who will be able to communicate with you better and, in general, make work more enjoyable.

Don't be fooled. The young managers already on board do not want more competition for upper-level managerial jobs. (There is only so much room for young Turks in any organization.) These managers will only bleed you dry for your talents and efforts, so that by the time you would be eligible for a higher-level position you will have burned out.

On the other hand, older managers might look on you as a son or daughter. They tend to tire of rubbing shoulders with the same old farts in their own age bracket all the time. Young people make them feel younger, and they like to fantasize that they are younger and more attractive than they really are. They are much more likely to give you awards simply to encourage you to stay around. They also believe it is easier for young people to respect and idolize them, since they regard young people as more naive.

† Avoid family-run businesses. You will never be able to aspire to a top-level executive position in these organizations. However, if any of the top family owners/executives have mar-

riageable children—the uglier the better—it might be a good move.

† Always check out the benefit package of an organization. You will not achieve a top-level, high-paying executive position in only a couple of years, even by applying the counsel in this handbook. Benefit packages in some companies and in the government can run as high as or higher than one third of the salary offered. Another, albeit unadvertised, benefit in government is that it is almost impossible to be fired. (A genuine Machiavellian doesn't usually worry about such things; but, hey, nobody's perfect.)

† Companies and government agencies with overseas offices or missions offer opportunities not only for adventure but also for valuable overseas contacts. Some of the contacts might prove a means for future employment by foreign companies or governments, often at much higher pay than what stateside employment can offer. And don't overlook contacts with the underworld or criminal element in these countries; mob-connected organizations are where the real power is in many places, some not far from home.

The advantage of making overseas underworld contacts is that you needn't risk interacting with them unless you really want to, since they will be far removed from you geographically through most of your career. Second, such contacts are much more difficult for U.S. law-enforcement agencies to track. However, you shouldn't need the services of the underworld if you successfully apply the concepts in this handbook. On the other hand, if you get yourself into an apparently impossible situation, who knows what sort of assistance you might need?

† A few words of advice you will never be given in a traditional job-placement training course. To begin with, at the first opportunity in a job interview, get the interviewer to relate his or her academic and organizational history to you. This will greatly assist you in determining the "correct" responses to subsequent interview questions. (Usually the higher the interviewers are in the organization, the more they like to talk about themselves.)

Second, ask the interviewer this question: If I were your child (or sibling, depending on the age of the interviewer), what would you tell me about the organization, and what should I really know? This might shake the interviewer's conscience to the foundation, and allow you to glimpse reality. If the interviewer complies with your request, a bond may be created between the two of you, since telling the naked truth is usually avoided in organizations, particularly in interviews.

Third, if you are interviewed in the interviewer's office, observe the decor. Are there pictures of children? You love children, of course. Does the interviewer have a picture of the spouse? How attractive or pleasant the spouse looks! What a handsome family! Are there awards or certificates on the office walls? My, how impressive! Are there plants in the office? You love plants and have many yourself. You get the idea.

Fourth, if you are introduced to someone who would be a coworker, get his home telephone number and ask permission to call after hours. When you do, ask him to relate any organizational problems he has encountered and whether it is likely that you will have to face the same challenges yourself. If you are lucky, your new acquaintance might also give you a dose of reality.

Finally, take a concealed tape recorder with you to the interview. If you are not offered a job, ask the interviewer please to reconsider, since you believe the interview was not conducted properly and you will, if necessary, be sending a transcript of the interview, together with a letter objecting to the manner in which it was conducted, to the interviewer's supervisor. If you are a member of a minority group or a woman, mention that you will also be sending a copy of the tape and your letter to the organization's Equal Employment Opportunity office.

(Machiavellianism is an equal-opportunity

adventure. Indeed, certain tactics that have traditionally put some people at a disadvantage in the business arena may in the Machiavellian world be nothing less than Very Heavy Artillery—reverse discrimination?)

2

SUBVERSION:
HOW TO BEGIN YOUR
CAREER WHEN YOU'RE
LOW MAN ON THE
TOTEM POLE

*. . . one ought never to allow a disorder to
take place in order to avoid war, for war is
not thereby avoided, but only deferred to
your disadvantage.*

THROUGHOUT YOUR CAREER, with rare excep-
tions, you should always regard your colleagues
as enemies. Especially at the beginning of your
career as a Machiavellian Manager, your colleagues are your greatest threat to promotion.
Friendship is a fine thing in its place, but on the
job everyone is a potential cutthroat. Of course,

you will want to treat everyone on the job in a friendly manner; having others recognize your hostility toward them will only hurt your cause.

Keep in mind that most first-line supervisors are chosen from the ranks, or nonsupervisory work force. You need not worry about dumb or even average colleagues. You do need to worry about the above-average and, especially, the intelligent and ambitious colleagues.

The first-line supervisory position and staff in any organization form the base unit for production or services. At this level production or service is important to the organization, and should be important to you as well. Hope that you will not find yourself in an organization whose survival depends on increased production, services, and quality improvement. If you do, you will have to work harder in an organizationally productive manner, something you will want to avoid as soon as the situation permits.

In any normally healthy organization such hard work will be unnecessary and, more important, perhaps even detrimental to your rapid advancement. Expending considerable effort on productive activities will reduce the amount of time and energy you have to devote to the Machiavellian Management tactics in this handbook. Furthermore, unnecessary hard work, far from being its own reward, can increase stress and tension, adverse conditions you must avoid. (It is quite sensible to cause in others those conditions, which you can advantageously control and direct.)

To organizations that are not themselves struggling for survival, apply the following rules:

† Produce only average, acceptable work that is stress-free for yourself and the organization. This will convey the impression to your colleagues and management that you are dependable, easy to get along with, nonthreatening, and well balanced.

† Always volunteer for special projects, and be alert for and ready to do any favor the supervisor requires. Special projects and favors (especially personal ones—the more personal the better) are always more important than the normal functions of the unit. They give you much more organizational visibility and help ingratiate you with management.

† Be very sociable with your supervisor. Make him think you respect him as an individual, not just as a supervisor, even if you deem him a jerk.

† Encourage the ambitious or intelligent colleague to engage in high-risk and potentially stressful activities that will, you hope, result in his making organizational enemies. If the colleague has assumed responsibility for multiple activities or developed programs, pick one that

is not stressful and is well accepted by management and urge your supervisor to transfer it to you. Explain to your supervisor that the colleague is overworked and that you would like to shoulder some of the burden. Finally, try character assassination. Most colleagues resent a high achiever. Exploit such resentment.

† Remember at this early stage of your career and throughout your rise to higher levels that management positions are given to good followers, not to good leaders. Avoid demonstrating good leadership, which implies independence of thought and willingness to take the initiative. Such characteristics in underlings are very threatening to upper-level management.

† If you have been out sick for an extended period or absent from work because of a death in your family, and your office sends you flowers or a nice card with a gift, you will naturally want to send a thank-you note. Remember, it is the person to whom you send the card that is important. Always address it to the head of the organization if members throughout the organization contributed, or to the head of the division if only members of the division contributed. Do so even if the head did not sign the card or make a contribution, or if you discover he made only a puny one. The head will then distribute the note to the staff rather than your supervisor or

some other lower-level manager within the organization.

This will have several advantages for you: It will help identify you to an important manager; it tells the manager he is important; and he will be pleased that you sent it to him personally with the heading "and Staff."

He in turn will have the advantage, when distributing your note to the staff, of reinforcing his authority and creating the impression that he truly cares about his employees' welfare. (Machiavellian Managers love to get credit for something they don't deserve.)

† It is always helpful to know how fast information travels within an organization. To check out your own company's "rumor dispersal quotient," simply plant an outrageous rumor and see how long it takes to get back to you. And occasionally plant a rumor about your company within a competing or outside agency to see how quickly the communication returns to your organization. Once you have established how efficiently your rumor mill works, use it to your advantage by sometimes planting competing rumors to keep your organizational competitors and enemies confused.

† As they say in real estate, location is an important consideration. Try to get yourself assigned to an office as close to a manager's office as you can. (The higher level the manager, the

better.) This will allow you to be seen often by management. It will also allow you to observe traffic into and out of the manager's office. When you can, position yourself so that you can overhear the manager's conversation. Some commercial spy stores carry state-of-the-art listening devices that you might consider using.

† Emphasize to your supervisor that you personally believe that true managerial characteristics—which he or she possesses, of course—are to you as important as, if not more important than, the technical work of the organization. Management courses have been preaching for years that organizations often make the mistake of promoting highly competent, technically oriented specialists to management positions. These so-called management experts assert that such highly qualified employees lack the "right stuff" for management positions. As a result, this advice has often backfired, and many marginally competent, if not downright incompetent, employees have been promoted to managerial positions over the last several decades. You should take advantage of these experts' stupidity and organizational gullibility.

† Volunteer to work overtime or after hours. When everyone else leaves the office, snoop around in neighboring offices or apply some of the nasty tricks related later in this handbook.

† Donate generously throughout your career to the organization's main charity drives. Give little or nothing to other charities or to your religious organization; they will not enhance your position within the organization.

On the other hand, by giving to your firm's charity drives you will reap recognition for your generosity, either in the form of a plaque or a personal letter from the top-level executive. Top-level management will deem you unselfish, caring, and generous, even though you aren't, of course.

One more tip. In some organizations you can fill out a pledge card that calls for a certain amount to be deducted from your pay. Check and see whether that can be changed later. If so, consider grossly overpledging. Later, quietly visit the pay office and explain that a recent family tragedy has resulted in unexpected expenses that require you, alas, to revise your pledge downward. By that time the good will has been done, and if you are found out, the same "tragedy" will avail for explanation.

After successfully applying these time-tested strategies, you should find yourself within one to three years at most as a first-line supervisor.

3

STRATEGIES FOR THE FIRST-LINE SUPERVISOR

For among other evils caused by being disarmed, it renders you contemptible; which is one of those disgraceful things which a prince must guard against. . . .

THE FIRST-LINE SUPERVISORY position is the testing ground to determine whether you have the potential to become a member of the "management team." Here you must demonstrate your conformity with and enthusiastic promotion of the goals and values of the team of high-level managers who control the organization.

The successful candidate for the first-level supervisory job must exhibit at least a satisfactory mastery of the knowledge, skills, and abilities necessary to the unit's function. That mastery, however, is not an important consideration for the first-line supervisor's advancement. Many would-be and never-to-be managers have never understood this difference. Other differences are described as follows:

† Determine which managers in your organization are the most powerful and who are the members of their cliques, that is, their supporters. In large organizations you will probably identify more than one of these power bases.

† Determine whether the middle manager to whom you report is a member of any of these power units and in what capacity or at what level. If a member, he is important to you. If not a member, he is but minimally important.

† If your middle manager is soon to retire or has a good chance of being promoted, apply the strategies you learned and used in Chapter 2 to get his job.

† If your middle manager is not a member of the management team and will not be leaving his position in the near future, either sabotage him to get him removed or transfer out. If you succeed in getting your middle manager removed, it would, of course, be ideal if you could get his position. However, if competition is keen and you think you cannot swing it, identify a well-qualified candidate either within your unit or, preferably, outside it, and promote his chances without your colleagues' knowledge.

If you transfer out, make sure you transfer to a position under a middle manager who either is a part of the management team or will be leaving.

† Consider expanding your search for a position to include nonsupervisory positions that have more promotion potential or a higher career ladder than supervisory posts. For example, many staff-support positions are designed to serve high midlevel and executive-level officers and are often titled staff assistant, program analyst, or management analyst.

† Always be present when one of your employees briefs higher-level management on a project or assignment, especially if the employee is competent. This gives upper-level management the impression that you're in charge, on top of things, and indispensable to and responsible for the employee's performance. Do not, of course, openly claim credit for your employee's success, but modestly acknowledge such credit if offered, even when undeserved, although in the latter case it is more discreet to do so out of hearing of your employee.

† If one of your employees produces a project or report that is in any way critical of a manager who can greatly benefit your career, inform the manager of what your employee has done and assure him that you "will take care of it."

Your behavior will have two advantages—it

will ingratiate you with the manager, and will demoralize the employee to the point that he will think twice in the future about criticizing one of your potential benefactors.

† If your upper-level managers despise or dislike one of your subordinates, make sure you give the employee a low performance rating. Never reward him, and in general try to make life miserable for him. Upper management will appreciate this and conclude that you are a team player, worthy of admission to the management team.

† Tell your employees that you're interested in them as individuals and encourage them to confide in you. Later, if necessary, use the information thus received to intimidate, blackmail, or stab them in the back.

† If you have an opportunity either to promote one of your own employees or to hire someone from the outside, always choose the latter. If you promote one of your own employees, that employee will undoubtedly be grateful to you, but not long. Next year he will ache for another promotion or some other organizational bennies, and if he doesn't get it, he will not only no longer be grateful, but probably be resentful, believing you have "turned" on him.

On the other hand, if you hire someone from

outside as a favor to a high-level manager or executive, that boss will be grateful for a much longer period. More important, he will look kindly on granting you more awards and promotions for having done him that favor.

† Never doubt your qualifications for a higher-level management position, no matter how complicated the programs to be managed may be. All you need do to appear very knowledgeable and qualified for a position of this kind is to play the Devil's advocate—always tactfully challenging whatever is submitted or proposed to you by subordinates. A simple "Why are we doing this?" spiced with a tinge of sarcasm will evoke lengthy explanations that will have you up to speed in no time. Once you understand what is going on, be magnanimous in your praise, and jocular: "Just want to keep you people on your toes."

This classic approach has been used successfully by thousands of managers of complex as well as relatively simple programs, managers who possess only minimal technical knowledge of the program area. Of course, never place yourself in a position where you must actually produce a product yourself or, almost as bad, make a proposal of your own to higher-level management. Avoiding such tasks is not difficult, since in most organizations decisionmaking is considered a top-management prerogative.

† If you wish to stick a competent employee on your staff with a bad performance rating, identify any of his coworkers who are friends and could be supportive of that person. Give those employees higher-than-usual, if not outstanding, performance ratings. This will make it very difficult for those employees to support the employee you are shafting. Another psychological boon: those employees will feel good about themselves when they realize their more competent colleague received a lower rating than did they.

† Establish one important habit at this point in your development as a Machiavellian Manager, and continue it throughout your career—edit your subordinates' writings at every opportunity. Keep in mind that, even if you are faced with a perfectly written draft, every sentence ever written can be rewritten without changing the substance. The only rule is, attempt to change smaller words to longer and loftier words—which look more impressive, even though they may mean the same thing. (*Lucky* to *fortunate*, and *nearby* to *accessible* are good examples.)

This practice, sometimes styled wordsmithing, is perhaps the most convenient and available means for showing your employees that you are indeed the boss. (Caution: Some obtuse managers get carried away and change the substance of a sentence and end up getting themselves in a wringer.)

† One very important skill a would-be Machiavellian Manager must develop is that of identifying subordinates who will both play by your rules and be no threat to you. It is ever helpful if not mandatory that you have life-and-death power over these persons' careers so that their loyalty to you is never in question. You will doubtless find one or more employees in your organization (they exist in every organization) who will gladly perform this task for you, and who may even suggest this strategy to you on their own.

Such employees are generally minimum performers and cannot expect to receive organizational and collegial respect based on their own professionalism and competence. As a result, in order not only to survive, but even to excel in the eyes of the organization, they resort to making themselves look good through backstabbing their more competent colleagues, using character assassination, and spying on coworkers and reporting their findings to their supervisors. They are the ones who brown-nose their bosses, not only in on-the-job areas by baking them birthday cakes but also outside the workplace— cutting their grass, repairing their cars, and the like. (Sound familiar?)

In any case, whether volunteered or recruited,

have one of those employees start "confidential" conversations about you in which he criticizes your leadership abilities, etc. The willingness of your agent to criticize will encourage others to follow suit, especially since the instigator is a person known to be close to you. Your toady can then mark those who jump into the fray with enthusiasm so that you can remove them at the first opportunity.

† Learn to identify quickly bright young employees who might or might not be an asset to you, depending on how they advance in the company. Smart employees quickly discover what is really going on in the organization and can be a threat to you. Call such persons in and share with them little secrets about others in the organization, and let them know that you have observed that they have already figured out these things. Then find a way to reward them with early promotions or other bennies. They will be grateful, but will also realize that you know how they think and that you will be keeping an eye on them. This tactic inspires at once admiration, loyalty, and fear, useful qualities to instill in your subordinates.

Timely application of these strategies should land you a midlevel managerial or senior-level staff position within three years.

4

STRATEGIES FOR
MIDDLE-MANAGEMENT
AND SENIOR-LEVEL STAFF
SUPPORT POSITIONS

*. . . you will always need the favour of
the inhabitants to take possession of a
province.*

MOST HARD-WORKING, COMPETENT, ethical, and
empathetic employees end their careers at this
plateau. Of course, they have probably taken
much longer to get to this stage in their careers
than you required.

As a successful Machiavellian Manager
you can now take a breather in your climb
up the organizational ladder since middle-
management and senior positions have a fair
amount of power, prestige, and salary attached

to them. This brief respite will afford you an opportunity to consolidate and strengthen your position and power unit within the organization as well as to develop your external power bases.

The latter activity is essential if you are to advance to an executive-level position, which, as a successful Machiavellian Manager, you surely wish to do. You are likely to find in your climb to the top that leverage must often be applied from outside an organization when internal channels are too well guarded. External connections can also provide a productive escape route on the off chance that things go awry in your quest.

The following rules should help you attain your ultimate goal of advancement to an executive-level position:

† Identify the strengths and weaknesses of the various management-team power units within your organization. Most of your energy will be spent dealing with the strongest and most influential of these power units. You can either ignore or divert for support to your own power unit the weaker units.

† Always give priority to assisting all of the strong power units when they seek your assistance, services, or cooperation. This will enable you to avoid disastrous power-unit struggles

within the organization, especially if all of them think you're their friend.

† Try to avoid supporting any single strong power unit if it makes an obvious bid or effort to wound or destroy another strong power unit. Be a mediating influence if possible. If this is not possible, stay neutral. This approach will give the top executive in the organization the impression that you are concerned about the welfare of the entire organization and that you are levelheaded.

† Give only the minimum necessary support to the less influential power units within the organization. It is also much safer to bargain or get favors from these less influential units in return for your providing them with the minimum necessary services, since you are bargaining from a position of strength.

† Deal personally with the managers of the other power units in matters of special requests, favors, and problems between you. If another manager is too angry to meet with you or thinks he is too busy to do so, don't be put off—deal with his top assistant. Your offer to meet with the other manager (in his office) or with his top assistant (also in his office) will show that you are deeply concerned about the situation and sincerely desirous of being helpful. By your initiating such meetings and going

to your opponents' offices, they will gain the erroneous impression that you possess humility.

† Identify the important power bases outside your organization. In government they include congressional committees and subcommittees that deal with your agency, and, of course, your own congressman and senators. In private business, they might include the board of directors, large shareholders, and an owner of the business who is not an active member of the on-site management team.

† Make contact with these extraorganizational power bases. If possible, involve yourself in job-related activities with these power bases. (Never send a subordinate.) If you cannot interact personally, at least try to do so with their staffs. They might then open the door to their bosses or at least inform their bosses of your existence and your willingness to cooperate with them.

† If job-related contact with the extraorganizational power bases is not feasible, then identify their social activities and socialize with them.

† Considering the attractiveness of the stakes, you should now consider a somewhat clichéd but nevertheless effective ploy: marry the top executive's daughter. If you're married already, be not deterred. Just see to it that your divorce is not messy.

A word of caution: do not use this strategy earlier in your career; the personal sacrifice you might have to make would not be worth the benefit—it might even get you stuck at a lower-management level.

If the top executive is not in favor of your marrying his daughter, consider getting her pregnant. This once strong and effective argument for marriage has been somewhat eroded in recent years, but top executives tend to be old-fashioned, even if their daughters are not.

† Give, or at least recommend, awards—from simple letters of commendation to more generous ones like fancy plaques and cash bonuses—to "worthy" employees outside the organizational unit you manage. As a middle manager you will have such opportunities. Identify those managers or their favorite employees who can most assist you in reaching your career goals and make awards to them as often as you can without being too obvious about what you are up to. Even if their support to your department has been only minimal, or merely within their normal job requirement, or even if their performance has been subpar, make the award anyway.

Most people who receive awards don't deserve them, so you might as well follow that common trend. But do it in a way that will bring maximum rewards to yourself in the long run. That's what awards are for—to reward those who deserve it, and you, of course, do.

† A most persuasive way to show your fellow managers that you are entitled to be a worthy member of the management team is to impress it with your prowess in problem solving in the team's behalf. You'll find this particularly handy when an audit team comes in and the management team, or a sizable part thereof, looks as if it might end up with egg on its face.

The key to this kind of situation is—identify the solution first and then define the problem, not vice versa. (If you can't identify a problem, it's no trick for a true Machiavellian Manager to create one.)

The solution to an audit of the kind described above is to select a lower-level employee in the organization who was associated in one way or another with the program or project being audited and to make that employee a scapegoat on behalf of the management team. Every good organization at times needs a sacrificial lamb on the altar for the "good of the organization."

This tactic is particularly effective if the employee in question has left the organization and is no longer around to defend himself. It will even work if the person was a high-level employee, provided he is now gone.

† Never report bad news on a project or program to your superiors. There is no sense expos-

ing your dirty laundry. Bad news of that kind, like a well-known substance, generally prefers to flow downhill. No sense upsetting the natural order of things.

Chances are your superiors will never have time to delve into your program area in detail, and what they don't know or what you choose not to tell them, will not hurt them, at least now. Ignorance is bliss.

It is wise, however, to complain occasionally to higher-level management about a certain employee or two, just in case your superiors eventually become aware of screwups in your program. In fact, it is essential that you identify at least one employee on your staff whom you can use as a fall guy. (Pregnant women and males who sometimes drink too much generally make good choices.)

These preselected underachievers will then be available to you as ready-made scapegoats. They will also provide you with the means of letting your bosses know that you had indeed warned them of these program problems in advance in the context of the employees you had complained about. Just make certain your initial complaints are vague enough that no action can be taken at the time; you don't want those people removed before the need arises.

On the other hand, always report good news about your program or project accomplishments to your superiors. Exaggerate as much as you think you can get by with. Make sure that upper management realizes that these program achievements could never have happened without your personal intervention.

† Once you are accepted into the management team, understand that there is a golden rule in some organizations that can never be broken—support the management team at all costs. Break that rule and you will doubtless find yourself downgraded to a lower position or even fired. Therefore, never criticize other team members to nonmembers. And when a team member finds himself in hot water, even if thoroughly deserved, you must support him—even if it involves a coverup.

The management team is always concerned that if one member goes down the tubes, it will besmirch the management of the entire organization. As a Machiavellian Manager you can take advantage of these crises, but you must be exceedingly careful.

† If you wish to create stress in a competitor by slandering and abusing him, make certain you do so in private, where there are no witnesses. If the person you are slandering is a nonsupervisory employee or a supervisor lower on the totem pole than you, you needn't worry about countercharges. After all, who in management would believe the word of a no-account nonsupervisory employee over the word of a su-

pervisor, or the word of a low-level supervisor over yours?

On the other hand, if the employee you are slandering is a supervisor on the same level as you, make sure that the person is not as highly regarded as you are by the management team. If the supervisor bellyaches about how you have treated him, simply accuse the pest of being paranoid, if not a downright liar. However, never attempt this tactic if the other supervisor is equally favored, or more highly favored than you, by the management team.

† As you will, at this level, be receiving reports from your subordinate units, reorganize them. Any report can be reorganized, even as it can be edited, a task you learned as a first-level supervisor. Don't worry about having to explain or justify to your subordinate employees what you are doing.

Check carefully your current position description. If like 99 percent of the other managerial position descriptions, it will inform you that you need not justify to your subordinates anything you do as long as it isn't illegal, dangerous to their health, or immoral. (Since in our rapidly evolving world definitions of *immoral* are changing daily, you may not even have to worry much about that category.)

Such liberty, of course, is a most appropriate and deserved reward for becoming a member of the management team. Your own superiors will confirm your right, and take on faith your legitimate need, to reorganize these reports.

In addition, keep changing your mind about the report's organization. This will cause the author(s) to make continual revisions and will eventually exhaust and demoralize him. Before long the author(s) will make a stupid mistake, which will allow you to bash him, give him a low performance evaluation, and garner for yourself all the credit for the final report.

† Be alert for projects you can cancel. Naive employees in your organization will ever be looking for ways to increase profits or services, thinking this will help them gain recognition and rewards. These initiatives usually involve up-front costs.

Cancel each of them, unless it is your idea, of course. You can then modestly reveal that you saved the organization sizable costs by canceling the "half-baked" or ill-considered projects or initiatives. You may even receive an organizational bonus for your cost-saving efforts.

† Start projects of your own that you know will require much expansion and more resources later on. Don't let anyone in on this. After the organization has invested a fairly large amount of money in your project, announce that the project will still require a generous infusion of funds to succeed.

The organization now has one of two choices: cancel the project and lose its initial investment, or provide you with the additional resources. Explain that neither you nor anyone else in the management hierarchy knew that the project would require this additional investment when it was first started. This way, upper management has to share the blame if it decides to cancel the project. If it doesn't cancel, you will have succeeded in greatly enhancing your empire.

By applying the above rules, you should be able to achieve an executive-level position within five to six years. Should you succeed in marrying the top executive's daughter, however, it could take much less time.

5

THE PRINCE:
THE SUCCESSFUL
MACHIAVELLIAN
EXECUTIVE

Further, the ruler of a foreign province as described, should make himself the leader and defender of his less powerful neighbours, and endeavour to weaken the stronger ones, and take care that they are not invaded by some foreigner not less powerful than himself.

CONGRATULATIONS! YOU'VE MADE IT. What is essential now is that you keep the position you have worked so hard to attain. In other words, your challenge is to maintain the status quo within the organization. You should create an environment that will allow you to sit back and enjoy the fruits of your labor with minimum stress and strain.

Now is also time to start thinking about and planning for your retirement—in luxury, of course. But just in case you miss the old excitement, here are some suggestions to liven up things a bit, as well as ensure your successful completion of a brilliant career at the top:

† Make sure that no one power unit in your organization achieves dominance for too long a time. Temporary dominance is all right, though it is even better if short-term dominance is shared with another power unit. Long-term dominance by any one unit is dangerous for you; it might effect drastic organizational changes—meaning your replacement.

† Always keep the strong power units off balance. When one strong power unit is obtaining too much influence, throw your support to another strong unit, but use only a minimum amount of your power to accomplish this.

† Keep the other strong power units happy by continuing to support them in the manner described in Chapter 3. After all, you do want to be able to enjoy your success.

† Volunteer your services for goody-goody programs or activities of the organization. Seek out positions with titles like Handicap Coor-

dinator, Equal Employment Opportunity Counselor, and United Fund Campaign Manager. Too, take on the responsibility of the company picnic, the Christmas party, and the like. You will, of course, delegate the real work involved to members of your staff or, failing that, hire a caterer (with company funds, naturally).

You will assume the glamour chores, like making announced appearances for the kickoffs, and presenting awards or prizes. At these you will properly thank those who did all the work. If you are gracious enough, and strike just the right tone of modesty, people will assume you did the real work yourself and give you all the credit.

† Determine where you want to retire. By now you will have accumulated considerable worldly goods. It would be improvident of you to pay for the transfer of these goods, along with the transportation costs of you and your family, to your ideal retirement location. Try to effect a transfer to a field office within commuting distance of your retirement villa. When all your expenses have been paid for by the organization, you can shortly retire.

† If you hear any murmurs of a guilty conscience after you retire—your conscience should be immune to such troubling interruptions by now—join your local church, synagogue, mosque, temple, or whatever, and there

become, of course, a high-level official. If religious life does not appeal to you, consider a civic organization. Many serve quite nicely as low-key retirement havens for Machiavellians who are not ready to abandon the skills they have so carefully honed over the years.

† Give thought to entering the political arena. Herein you can make the ultimate use of your Machiavellian skills. Double talk is an especially prized skill among politicians.

† On the other hand, if you would rather go out with a bang rather than a whimper, you can—guess what?—*reorganize.* Reorganization is one of the most common phenomena associated with newly appointed top-level executives. Most of them know that by reorganizing they send a strong message throughout the organization and to those outside it that there is a new man in charge. (It really doesn't matter to most top executives that no substantive improvements in productivity will result from their reorganization.)

A wise Machiavellian Manager also realizes that reorganization can enhance his power. When reorganizing, make sure you place your organizational enemies and strong competitors in charge of inconsequential units. By so doing you neutralize them in one masterful stroke. Then you can reward those employees who came to pay you homage and congratulate you on your appointment by placing them in the organizational power units.

† One way to ensure survival as a Machiavellian executive if, God forbid, you are caught with your hand in the cookie jar, is to develop and keep a black book on all your fellow executives. Most of them won't know of the specific and legal constraints placed on your program area. Thus, when a fellow executive asks you to do something that you know to be a prohibited or an illegal action in order to support one of his program initiatives, tell him that it is risky, but that you will go along with it. This will make him grateful for your flexibility.

Then write a memo to your file that you were ordered to take this action, or that you felt your career would be in jeopardy if you didn't agree. Also, be certain to mention in your memo to the file that you strongly voiced your objection to the other executive, but that your objection was ignored or overruled. You thereby ensure that any contemplated disciplinary or adverse action against you will not result in anything drastic, like a salary reduction or being fired, for fear that you might spill the beans on other executives in the organization. (The late J. Edgar Hoover of the FBI was notorious for his black book on the lives of powerful and influential congressmen and other high-level government officials, perhaps even including a president or two.)

† Take advantage of a recession. An economic downturn, especially a prolonged one, can offer wonderful opportunities for a top-level executive to consolidate his power and increase his personal wealth at the same time. Even if your organization is not suffering greatly under a recession (statistics are created to be manipulated), it offers you the excuse to fire numerous midlevel managers.

When you were appointed to your top-level executive position you most assuredly inherited many midlevel managers whose loyalties were to others in the organization and who might even have been active supporters of your enemies. All you need do in a recession to get rid of them all is to abolish their positions. Later, after a decent interval, reestablish those positions and fill them with loyal lap dogs.

This strategy has two immediate advantages for you: first, it eliminates the present threat to your preeminence; second, it enhances your power base. There may be even a third advantage: a bonus check for your temporary cost-saving action.

Your strategy may also result in a financial bonanza for you outside the organization. The midlevel managers you have fired are doubtless strong middle- to upper-middle-class families, and like most people in their class, they have high mortgage payments. They will find it almost impossible to meet these payments and their other bills and will probably be living on unemployment benefits.

Since banks will usually foreclose on a mortgage after three months of missed payments, let the people you have fired sweat for about two or two and a half months, then contact them. Explain graciously that you feel terrible about what has happened to them and offer to buy their houses for just a few dollars above what they paid for them, or, if times are really bad and you can get away with it, for substantially less than what they paid. You will very likely be wiping out their life savings, but you will be saving them from an even greater disaster, which is something you want to emphasize. You will not only grow richer from doing this, but also probably be doing a favor for the human race, for, said Darwin, only the fittest deserve to survive anyway.

Finally, your actions, in toto, will have the advantage of creating among the remaining employees in the organization abject fear about their own job security. They will know that their survivability is ensured only at the price of unquestioning loyalty to you.

† You should always allow your employees to abuse one or two agency or company privileges. The word will soon get around, and sooner or later everyone will be doing it, including your enemy. Once your enemy has joined the crowd,

stomp on him vigorously. Announce to the rest of the staff that an employee has been identified who flagrantly violated agency or company privileges and that you have taken appropriate disciplinary action to keep this abuse from happening again.

Two common examples of abuse that easily lend themselves to disciplinary action are: misuse of leave privileges and enriching oneself by cashing in first-class airline tickets and flying business or economy class.

Your strategy has these advantages for you: (1) it punishes your enemy; (2) it will immediately cow all your employees into compliance with the rules, making you look good; and (3) it will strike terror in the rest of the subordinates, who will think, There but for the grace of God go I.

† Develop a large bladder. As a top-level executive you will need it, for you will attend important meetings at which votes will be taken on matters that could affect your position and power. Such meetings tend to drag on and on.

Therefore, if you haven't yet achieved your admirable goal, be sure to use the bathroom just before the meeting starts. Then when your competitors or enemies must excuse themselves to answer nature's call, propose alternatives to their suggestions and pass them in their absence.

† If you and your management team have messed up badly, and you must make a public

announcement to that effect, assign the responsibility to a subordinate manager. You are in the public mind, to be associated only with success in your organization. When things get better, then you can make public announcements.

† If you must lay off a large number of employees (usually as a result of your own incompetence), do not immediately identify the organizational units and plants that will be closed or otherwise affected. Your vagueness will make your employees everywhere work even harder so as not to lose their own jobs, each one hoping it will be the other guy instead.

This has two advantages for you. First, the extra effort exerted by all might compensate, at least in part, for your own blunders. Second, you can make an announcement to those not laid off that your own unflagging efforts (here, as above, be elusive) resulted in fewer layoffs than earlier anticipated. Those who retain their jobs will be eternally grateful to you.

† If you must fire someone high up in your organization who has a high public profile, merely announce that the high-level executive has turned in his resignation and that you have, regretfully, accepted it. Be generous in your praise of the chap and express your utmost confidence that he will go on to excel in other fields.

You can get by with this by insisting that all high-level executives turn in a resignation letter to you as a cost of being selected to their position, and that they do so with the understanding that you reserve the right to accept the resignation at any time (particularly when one stops playing the sycophant). To be safe, have one of your lawyers draw up an appropriate agreement for them to sign.

† One quality is indispensable for the top executive—*pizzazz*. Stockholders demand this characteristic in top-level executives of their companies more than any other trait. It is even more important than your ability to increase the strength of your company's sales and stock. (The U.S. automobile industry is a good example of this phenomenon. In spite of producing automobiles that for years Americans did not want, making inferior products, failing to invest in state-of-the-art technology and factory modernization, laying off hundreds of thousands of employees as a result of their own incompetence, the top executives have thrived. All are multi-millionaires. They "earn" multi-million-dollar salaries and receive millions more in benefits, even when they retire.) Stockholders relish identifying with a charismatic top executive. They feel important when they see his face on national television in ads and business profiles and on talk shows. These stockholders are, for the most part, white-collar or fairly wealthy individuals. They certainly don't want to be identi-

fied with base blue-collar workers, who, of course, help make their exalted status possible.

Thus, if you're really good at pizzazz and display this quality publicly, say, in "public service announcements" (advertising spots), you might even be asked to run for president.

† Give it your best effort to influence the process by which people are nominated for and selected to your company's board of directors. The people you really want on the board are those who have inherited their power, wealth, and prestige. (The last people you want peering over your shoulder are those who sweated their way to the top.)

You will gain two advantages from this. First, it allows for public recognition of these individuals and their families, who are associated with their success.

Second, such silk-stocking folk can relate only theoretically to your company's rank and file, who do the actual work. They certainly are above socializing privately with those grunts. And they, unlike working stiffs, don't have to worry about mortgages or car payments, the quality of public education, and having enough money to send their children to college or vocational schools.

You see, board members are concerned mostly with having enough after-tax dollars for salting away and for maintaining their lavish lifestyles and privileged status. They thus have little genuine sympathy for the rank and file and cannot really appreciate their needs. And they certainly cannot identify with them—they would find it mortifying ever to be identified with them.

Obviously, then, blue bloods will be much more inclined to ensure that you, as top dog, keep or even increase your organizational benefits. Even at the expense of the unfortunate souls under you.

† If by some fluke or miracle someone is nominated to the board of directors who actually has come up through the ranks of the organization, you must take an active role in ensuring that he will not be selected by the stockholders, unless he is readily willing to sacrifice his values. (It goes without saying that you must have your trusted subordinates dig up everything they can find out about the person. And in the likely event that something is discovered that can be blown out of proportion, then you are home free. Any good Machiavellian Manager knows how to blow things up.)

The hard-working nominee will not, of course, be intimidated by you. He knows you put on your pants the same way as everyone else in the organization, and thus will not be inclined to vote you an enormous salary and other valuable benefits, especially if the organization is doing poorly.

One way to ensure that this person is not elected by the stockholders is to see to it that the qualification statements of candidates made available to stockholders for making their choices are very restrictive. That is, limit these statements to such things as university degrees, high positions held in other organizations, service on boards of directors of other organizations, the many honorary societies and charities the candidate has been associated with or contributed to, and high-level advisory or honorary positions. Such qualifications—which proliferate among the right types—will make the person who came up through the ranks look like a drudge and a slacker by comparison.

This tactic will help keep your stockholders uninformed about the true qualifications that should be associated with selection to a board of directors. You certainly don't want an informed stockholder electorate. Ignorance is bliss, and it allows you to continue on your merry Machiavellian way.

Part II

SHARPENING YOUR SWORD: REFINING YOUR SKILLS

6

SUBTERFUGE: YOUR APPROACH TO TRADITIONAL MANAGEMENT THEORIES, PRINCIPLES, AND PRACTICES

But it is necessary to be able to disguise this character well, and to be a great feigner and dissembler. . . .

CONTRARY TO THE assertions of modern-day pundits of management theory that new techniques and approaches to management have recently been developed in our business schools, the body of knowledge on management theory has stayed essentially the same since the early sixties. Since that time, the only changes have been, for the most part, cosmetic, variations on a theme—putting old wine into new bottles—and have involved plagiarism in the extreme.

According to the traditional model, the effective manager must strive for mastery of these areas: planning, organizing, directing and motivating, staffing, and controlling. All of this learning is to be directed toward increasing the quality of the organization's products and the efficiency of its services.

The traditional approach has aided only a privileged few in obtaining promotions. And the privileged few who do manage to advance using these methods do so at a snail's pace, compared to the meteoric rise of the Machiavellian Manager.

Here are a few alternative models that will work for you:

† Planning, organizing, directing and motivating, staffing, and controlling are all primarily maintenance activities, and you should give them no priority whatever. Provide direction in these areas only to the extent that your efforts will either strengthen or secure your position. For example, hire only employees who you think will be loyal to you, and who are competent, but not so competent as to be a threat to you. And reward only those employees who are loyal to you.

† Delegate the above management functions to a competent staff member, but retain your approval authority. These functions entail hard work, and their implementation will not lead to rapid promotion. They become important to you only if there is a screwup; then they attract high-level management attention. When this happens you must take personal charge. Put all the blame on your subordinates.

On the other hand, when the subordinate does good work on these projects, throw him a bone or two. Give him a high performance rating or an occasional award, especially one he might hesitate to accept, like an unauthorized extra week of vacation.

† Give lip service to the traditional management approaches. Whenever the opportunity arises, affirm your belief in and support of the traditional management theories. Pick up a few stock management texts (used copies at a college bookstore will suit your purposes), select a few fancy phrases, and quote them liberally on suitable occasions. Be sure to add a skeptical word or two so your listeners will understand that you consider no textbook theory "the last word." You are, in other words, a step or two ahead of even the most prestigious business schools.

This technique is a most effective way of misleading your competitors into thinking they know how you operate, and gives your top management the impression that you care about your employees and the organization.

And, by all means, prominently display those traditional management books in your office—the used copies will work fine. They will show that you were frugal even as a student.

† Never worry about sanctions unless you foul up badly. Be comforted with the realization that it is extremely rare, almost unheard of, for a manager to be criticized—certainly not in his performance rating—for not meeting his planning or production milestones, for overspending his budget, or for losing one or more employee grievance cases. Should you find yourself in a situation in which fingers seem to be pointing at you, be generous—spread the blame around, something true Machiavellians know how to do instinctively.

† Never volunteer for productivity or quality improvement programs. If your organization gets involved in such a program, delegate that responsibility to a subordinate if you are required to participate. Instruct the employee you assign to manipulate statistics so that you can demonstrate increased productivity or quality improvement without having to do anything different. Assure the toady that you will protect him no matter what. If the lid blows off, he can be left "twisting in the wind."

† If you need an easy and effective way to increase company profits or to cut back costs in a budget squeeze without taking any skin off your own back, simply get rid of employees. Target employees who are not sufficiently loyal to you and who have only a minimum effect in boosting your career aspirations. For instance, employees near retirement. Merely tell them that the workload has lightened and that you need to release them only temporarily. Then never rehire them. This will effect a considerable cost saving, since these employees will not be paid salaries or provided with health benefits, and the company will not later have to bear the cost of their retirement.

After you have cleaned house, inform a few key employees that you have got rid of "deadwood," which tack will make you seem less heartless, and a good, efficient manager. Employees left behind will then be willing to take up the slack so as not to be deemed more deadwood. Moreover, hint that the money saved will go toward raises for employees who can produce more. When those raises are not forthcoming, simply blame upper-level management or perhaps the stockholders.

Your action may even garner you a productivity improvement award and a considerable cash bonus.

To play it safe, though, and to avoid possible lawsuits, fabricate evidence against the employees you intend to fire and place it in their files. Get younger employees to assist in this effort by offering awards or bonuses for ferreting out inefficiencies or sabotaging the targeted victims' work. (Enthusiastic young employees can always come up with information about how older employees aren't doing their jobs—this makes more room for them.) Of course, you will not be too specific about when the rewards for such actions will materialize.

† The only important consideration in your own performance rating is whether your supervisor likes you or fears you. Anything in between will not produce a high performance rating for you.

† Carefully consider using first names when dealing with superiors. Although usage of first names is widely accepted today, be prudent and ask permission. When it is granted, continue for a time to use the person's last name—a sure sign that you have too much respect for the person to take advantage of his generosity.

On the other hand, in conversations with others always refer to the person as "Jim" or "Art," thus conveying that you are on close terms with the powers above.

7

SUCCESSFUL SABOTAGE TECHNIQUES

A prince being thus obliged to know well how to act as a beast must imitate the fox and the lion, for the lion cannot protect himself from traps, and the fox cannot defend himself from wolves.

SABOTAGE TECHNIQUES ARE a very important tool for the Machiavellian Manager but should be used only as a last resort. Sabotage most often needs to be applied to three sorts of employee: (1) the colleague who is intelligent and ambitious; (2) the manager who refuses to die or retire, blocking your advancement opportunities; and (3) the employee at any level who possesses high standards of integrity. The last group constitutes a danger to you only if it recognizes the strategies and techniques you are employing and is able to prove its observations.

Some ways to handle the intelligent and ambitious colleague have already been described in Chapter 2. Here are a few additional methods of undermining those who may seem a threat to you.

† Seek opportunities to communicate and work directly with your manager's boss. Whenever your manager's boss expresses his dissatisfaction with your own boss, readily agree, while making it clear that you do so with reluctance. (The Machiavellian never seems overeager to do anything.) State, furthermore, that you would never act in the same manner as your boss, but at the same time hint that your actions are hampered because your boss is your boss, after all, and loyalty is something you value and try to practice. Openly struggling with your conscience is a most impressive way of conveying the right impression.

However, if your manager's boss is willing to give you assignments directly, readily accept them, but always inform your own supervisor when this happens. This protects you with your supervisor and puts him in a bind at the same time. He must either complain to his boss, thus causing stress and tension, or let you act independently, allowing you to show him up.

† Identify strong power units that are enemies of your manager. Seek opportunities to communicate verbally with them. When they complain about your boss, listen attentively and be sympathetic. Relate to them your willingness to do anything you can to help smooth things over and to advance the designs of your manager's enemies.

This approach has two advantages for you: (a) it undermines your manager, and (b) it makes you a potential candidate for landing a good position with your manager's enemies.

† Become good friends with your own secretary and those of other managers. Encourage them to talk about their job frustrations. Be sympathetic, listen, and take them out to lunch occasionally, especially in pairs or groups, so that if you are seen you will not be suspected of open hanky-panky. Secretaries are gold mines of choice information, and are often inclined to talk more freely when their peers are present than when in private.

Try to get your superior's secretary to inform you of any irregularities in her boss's behavior, such as his leave record (managers are especially vulnerable in this area if they have recently experienced a divorce or a death in the immediate family), reimbursements for travel expenditures, his biases toward powerful managers within the organization, organizational maneuvers he is planning, and the like. Inform his enemies of these matters.

† Identify and cultivate other employees who are dissatisfied with their bosses. Prod them to share their grievances with you, and then impart this information to their managers. Be sure to express to them how wrong their employees' attitudes are and that you believe they are being unjustifiably abused. The managers will appreciate your concern and will suppose that you have much higher ethical standards than their own employees. They also might want to hire you if a promotional opportunity arises in their units.

† Hire an attractive nymphomaniac or, if you can't find one, a very sexy female employee who appears to be loose. Give her high ratings and top recommendations and get her transferred to your enemy's staff. Take care not to get too familiar with such women—many are themselves skillful Machiavellians and may be able to exploit your indiscretions to their benefit and your disadvantage. (On that note, being able to recognize other Machiavellian Managers is a valuable trait, but one that, if you carefully ponder the wisdom in this little volume, you will almost automatically assume.)

† Identify an activity that, if not performed correctly, will cause great embarrassment or seriously reduce your organization's profits. Give

your supervisor only partial information about the activity, get his authorization, and let the assignment proceed to self-destruct or fail. In the meantime, tell a few influential contacts of the factors you did not share with your supervisor, emphasizing that these factors were, indeed, made known to your supervisor.

You must also write a memo to the file stating that you discussed these factors with your supervisor and make sure that the memo is dated prior to the inevitable failure of the project. Make a few marks in the upper corner that could be your boss's initials and run the memo through the copy machine. Then successively make a copy of each copy until the marks are not quite clear enough for positive identification.

† Get on your competitor's personal computer when he is not attending it and send a nasty message to some other employee about the top executive, then "misdirect" it to the boss's PC. Consider also getting into your competitor's files and wiping out important documents about projects and assignments he has been working on. Be sure to do the same to the backup files on disks as well. (In anticipation of such efforts, begin as early as you can after joining a firm ferreting out code words for computer entry. They always come in handy.) Do not, however, resort to both tactics at the same time; your competitor may suspect foul play.

† If you feel threatened by a competent employee, you can easily sabotage his performance by setting totally unrealistic deadlines for completing projects. Competent subordinates are ever eager to prove their abilities to you. Their eagerness often manifests a tendency to being overoptimistic about and somewhat overconfident in what they can produce in a limited time frame.

When such an employee inevitably comes to you in distress to announce that he can't meet your deadline, you will graciously extend it, thus ensuring a quality product within a reasonable time frame.

After you get the product, give the employee a minimum or unsatisfactory rating for not meeting the original deadline, which will then enable you to claim the credit for the quality and the timeliness of the product.

† Another way to shaft an employee you don't like: assign him an activity that requires cooperating with other organizational components. Call up the managers in those units before the subordinate begins the assignment. Explain to them that this is a problem employee and apologize for having to assign him to the project, but since you were so short of staff you had no other choice. Request that they inform you if they have any problems with the person during the course of the assignment. This will

encourage the other component managers to complain about him and will give them a green light to dump on him anytime. Then use this adverse feedback to stick the employee with a bad performance rating.

✝ Learn to sabotage audits. Sooner or later you and your project or program will face an audit. One of the best ways to sabotage it is character assassination. Solicit the help of your fellow managers. Their programs might be involved in the same audit; if not, they know their turn will come.

All that you and your fellow managers need do is call the audit team's management and complain bitterly that the team members have a hidden agenda, that they are prejudiced, that their minds have already been made up, that they are rude and offensive, and that their interview style is one of interrogation. These charges will require the team's management to make intense inquiries into the activities of the audit team and perhaps even initiate a formal investigation into the charges.

All this will have the effect of delaying the audit, demoralizing and intimidating the audit team, and sapping its energy to the point where it will either back off or do a lousy job. If you're lucky, all the flack you and your fellow managers have caused might even get the audit canceled.

Finally, your efforts might even occasion support from an unexpected quarter. If there are any Machiavellians on the team, they are probably aching to take over the audit leader's position and might use your actions to assist them in enacting their own sabotage designs.

8

ASSIGNATION: SOCIALIZING TECHNIQUES

Let a prince therefore aim at conquering and maintaining the state, and the means will always be judged honourable and praised by everyone. . . .

WHEN YOU SOCIALIZE with a person it means you respect him and enjoy his company, since your decision to associate with him is obviously made by free choice. In the workplace you will see only an incomplete picture of your colleagues, and valuable information that you can use against one can be obtained when you socialize with him. Such contact will also mislead him into thinking that you value him as an individual of worth.

You, as a successful Machiavellian Manager, must mingle socially not only with those who can advance your career, but with your enemies as well. In the latter case, you will gain information not only to use against your enemy, but also to help disarm and confuse him.

The following tips will help you get into the social scene, where you can accomplish much:

† Become a member of your company's or agency's athletic teams and participate vigorously. You may have to invest a few dollars in golf or tennis lessons, but such investments usually pay off handsomely. Don't overdo it. You want only to become skillful enough to compete without embarrassment. You certainly don't want to beat anyone important.

Athletic activity has the additional advantage of enabling you to release your own stress.

† Identify the clubs to which your friends and enemies belong and join them. Become friends with your friends' friends as well as with your enemies' enemies.

† Join the same church, synagogue, mosque, temple, etc. Always appear to be devout in services and make sure your friend or foe observes this.

† Join activities to which your friends' or enemies' family members belong. Properly cultivated, family members can both help promote

your interests and provide you with damaging information.

† Get your children and spouse involved. Have them join athletic teams, bridge clubs, bands, and the like—any activity in which your potential benefactors, enemies, or their families participate. This will also open up opportunities for you to mingle with them as well.

† Be selective about the events you attend. You'll have opportunities galore to attend organizational birthday celebrations, promotion or transfer parties, retirement luncheons, and seasonal events like Christmas and New Years' parties. Determine whether the employees being honored at such events are important to your career or are favorites of managers who can influence your career, and whether the organization sponsoring the event may be a valuable asset to you. If so, attend the function. If not, forget it—don't waste your time.

By not attending no-account organizational functions you can create the impression among important managers—who generally feel duty-bound to drop in on such gatherings—that you would have liked to attend but were prevented from going because of pressing organizational business. Subordinates who are too busy for parties always impress higher-level bosses. Just be sure that you require all your own employees to attend so that your superiors will also know that you "take care of your people."

† Occasionally schedule a meeting at a very inconvenient time—late on Friday afternoon works well—and make attendance mandatory. There provide a nice spread of food and drink at your own expense (later reimburse yourself by padding an expense account), but serve the food after you have covered your "important" business. (Find some dish that you can easily prepare yourself and make certain everyone knows you made it with your own hands—it adds a nice touch.)

The net effect? Everyone will first grumble, and then feel guilty about having criticized your decision. Your subordinates will also be less likely to feel animosity toward you as you continue on your (Machiavellian) path. In addition, the word will get around to upper management that even in a crunch, albeit contrived, you go the extra mile to take care of your employees.

A word of caution. Don't try to implement every one of the above rules, since it would most likely become obvious what you are up to. *Selective* implementation of them should suffice for your purposes.

9

ESPIONAGE:
MAKING THE MOST OF
OFF-SITE CONFERENCES

*Nothing causes a prince to be so much
esteemed as great enterprises and giving
proof of prowess.*

OFF-SITE ORGANIZATIONAL CONFERENCES offer an
excellent opportunity for politicking, socializing, observing colleagues, and playing the nice
guy during conference sessions. Some managers
try to get out of these conferences or delegate
such duties to a subordinate. Never do this. To
skip a conference is to violate a basic rule of
Machiavellian behavior: Never pass up a chance
to improve your own position. Besides, attending a conference provides you with an excuse
later on for any screwup: "It must have happened when we were in Hawaii."

The following simple rules will help you make the most of any conference you decide to grace with your presence:

† Consider the conference agenda as trivia. Most conference agendas address the traditional management issues of planning, organizing, directing and motivating, staffing, and controlling, or perhaps some trendy topic lately hatched by a professor who has written seven books on management but never managed anything but a class of graduate students. The only thing you must be alert to is whether any part of the agenda threatens your power, prestige, and salary. In case it does, you must take an active, forceful role in the proceedings by subtly undermining anything that can work to your detriment. Otherwise, since you know traditional management approaches are, for the most part, meaningless to your rapid advancement, you can be Mr. Congeniality—always agreeable, cooperative, and apparently enthusiastic in your support of the conference agenda.

† Using the skills you have perfected by following the guidance in Chapter 8, socialize with those who can help you obtain your career goals. You will probably encounter underlings or no-accounts who will want to socialize with you during after hours, but avoid them as much as possible. In addition to being boring, they can

convey the impression that you aren't very clever in selecting company for after-hours activity. Always be, and be seen by others, in the company of the organization's elite.

† Be alert to any scandals, rumors, gripes, too much drinking, sexual liaisons, and the like, connected to anyone of importance. If something looks juicy, gather as much information about the incident from as many sources as you can without being too obvious. At the same time, subtly spread news of the incident, even if it is only a rumor.

† If you can be discreet, seduce an employee of your enemy. (Do not attempt this with an employee of a manager who can support your career goals.) Once seduced, the person can be of great use to you as a spy and an informer. Keep in mind, however, that she will always be a liability to you. You will have to treat her with caution or see to it that she eventually gets transferred out of your immediate vicinity or is fired.

† Volunteer to help organize the next conference. This accomplishes four things:

  a. It conveys the impression that you are concerned about and support the organization's goals and objectives.
  b. It helps you group your friends and enemies in a way most advantageous to you.

c. It permits you to create an agenda from which you will be the main beneficiary.
d. It gives you organizational exposure and will allow you to play a leadership role in the next conference.

10

DECEPTION: MAKING THE MOST OF TRAINING COURSES

A prince, therefore, ought always to take counsel, but only when he wishes, not when others wish. . . .

MANY HIGH-LEVEL MANAGERS try hard to avoid training courses. Most programs for high-level employees are management courses that attendees often find too theoretical or just plain boring. They already consider themselves experts, especially if they have had a management course, and they find these sessions too similar to previous ones they have attended, or too condescending, or irrelevant to their needs. They often maintain—and sometimes even believe—that they have no time for these courses.

You must not think this way. If you follow the rules below, you will find that training courses can be greatly advantageous to you.

† Volunteer or ask to be given training. This ploy gives upper-level management the impression that you are sincerely interested in personal growth. It also gives you the opportunity to apply the other rules in this section.

† Always choose the training course in which the highest level of management is to participate. Courses for employees at your level or below are a waste of time for you. Even if you are not qualified, based on the course criteria, for admittance to higher-level programs, get your boss to write a note that this is part of your career development plan. If that doesn't work with the training people (usually it will), ask them to put you on a substitute list.

† As you did with conferences, consider the course content trivia, especially if it is a management course. Management training courses have been preaching essentially the same doctrines since the early sixties. They address the traditional management theories and principles that, as you know by now, are only maintenance activities and will not help you get promoted rapidly.

† Once in the course, identify the highest level of managers or executives there. These

may be high-level officials within or not associated with your organization. Give first priority to those in your organization and second priority to those outside it. (All of these managers should be at least two grades or organizational levels above you.)

† Take advantage of what happens to the high-level managers during training courses. A funny thing happens to many people in management training programs—it is almost like getting religion or being born again, even if the phenomenon is short-lived. Being ordinary (not Machiavellian) managers, they are bored to death with their jobs and prospects, and suddenly they think they have found the Holy Grail of management technique. During this period of temporary euphoria, these high-level managers are vulnerable.

Therefore, give them as much recognition and attention as possible during the class sessions, fan their enthusiasm, validate their feelings of discovery. Socialize with them after class and encourage them to talk about how their newfound knowledge will help them solve problems, and how willing (and able) you would be to help them. If they wish only to pontificate, tell them how stimulating and original their ideas are and how privileged you would be to work for a manager "who sees things with the kind of insight you obviously have, Tom." (First names are perfectly acceptable to people on the plateaus of organizational ecstasy.) Given their high-level egos, most managers will love you for your attitude.

† Seize opportunities in class to massage managers' egos. Should an opportunity arise at the end of the course for stating what you have learned, or if the coordinators conduct an exercise calling for special recognition of class participants, be sure you point out the important contributions of any high-level managers in the class who can enhance your career goals, even hire you. Tell the class and instructor how perceptive and inspiring these participants were to you during the course.

† Exchange telephone numbers with these high-level managers. Ask if you may call them for their advice in solving organizational problems. (Seeking advice is a natural Machiavellian trait. It flatters people, and the advice can generally be ignored without the offerer being aware of it.) This will, after a decent interval, afford you the opportunity to approach them for employment or promotional opportunities. Even better, it gives them the opportunity to offer these benefits to you.

SUMMARY OF
PARTS I AND II

*Wherefore it is to be noted that in taking a
state its conqueror should weigh all the
harmful things he must do and do them
all at once so as not to have to repeat them
every day, and in not repeating them to be
able to make men feel secure and win
them over with the benefits he bestows
upon them.*

THE ADVICE CONTAINED in the foregoing
pages is by no means sufficient to analyze
completely the organizational behavior necessary to Machiavellian purposes. The true Machiavellian Manager knows instinctively much
of what has been presented, and more. He will
not find it necessary to overanalyze his circumstances; such ruminations he will leave for
graduate students, theoreticians, and others
who prefer pondering to acting.

The Machiavellian Manager is a doer, and after the fashion of the ancient prince, he does unto others before they can do unto him. Life is short, and to enjoy it he must get where he is going without being diverted by such pithy comments as, "Be sure to stop and smell the roses along the way." There are no roses along the path to success, only thorns. The Machiavellian Manager quickly learns how to blunt the thorns that tear at his progress and sees to it that the paths of others are similarly obstructed. One way he does that, while maintaining his benevolent posture, is to strew the paths of others with roses and encourage them to stop and sniff. While they are thus employed, he goes about his business.

One more point. If any one of the above recommendations seems too trivial to you, remind yourself that to the true Machiavellian, no crumb is too small to be consumed without benefit. As one famous Machiavellian once said, "Those who ignore the pebbles will have trouble swallowing the stones."

Part III

ENTERING INTO COMBAT WITH THE MACHIAVELLIAN MANAGER

OR

ESCAPING WITH YOUR SKIN

PREFACE

IF YOU HAVEN'T read Parts I and II of this handbook, Part III may not make much sense; understanding the mentality of the Machiavellian Manager is a must. Remember, never underestimate a Machiavellian Manager or Machiavellian senior staff assistant. To do so is fatal to your career and eventually to the organization. Everyone is subject to his manipulations, and he may be found anywhere in the organization. As long as there is anyone in your organization who is qualified by virtue of his position for your job, there exists the potential that he is a Machiavellian Manager. You must also remember that the true Machiavellian Manager is never satisfied with his position in the organization until he reaches the top. He will use any strategy and technique to exploit or undermine you to gain his advancement as long as he thinks he won't be caught.

This section will identify where the Machiavellian Manager is most vulnerable, and show how you can exploit his vulnerability by either neutralizing him or, even better, firing him. This is altogether possible because the Machiavellian Manager is, for the most part, totally unconcerned about the health of your organization, even though he will assert the opposite. Moreover, despite his skills, he will have made throughout his career many enemies whom you can enlist to help you.

In addition, most Machiavellian Managers are arrogant and consider their competition either naive or ignorant of their stratagems. Once you and your organization become aware of his existence, he loses much of his power.

You will also learn from this section survival strategies and techniques for the times when the Machiavellian Manager is so powerful and entrenched that you cannot compete with him.

Furthermore, you may, of course, employ the same strategies and techniques against the Machiavellian Manager that he himself uses, but you may find, according to your own values and beliefs, that many of them are unethical. Only your conscience can guide you. However, this section will provide you with what most people would consider the ethical means to survive, or to enter into successful combat with the Machiavellian Manager.

The following pages provide guidance and assistance to executives, middle managers, supervisory and nonsupervisory employees in dealing

with Machiavellian Managers—all are potential victims.

A word about the epigraphs in this part. Niccolò Machiavelli is best known for describing
successful strategies and techniques of some of
the more notorious princes of his time. Although his work was attacked on moral grounds
even in his own age, Machiavelli generally took
no moral positions on the actions he described;
he merely reported on what he had seen as a
career diplomat in the service of the Republic of
Florence. In addition to describing what we now
call "Machiavellian" practices, however, he
praised the behavior of those princes whom he
considered good and virtuous rulers. The epigraphs in this part are meant to reflect this as-
pect of his writing.

11

COUNTERCOUP: REVAMPING PERFORMANCE APPRAISALS, AWARDS, PROMOTION SYSTEMS, AND SALARY STRUCTURES

A prince must also show himself a lover of merit, give preferment to the able, and honour those who excel in every art.

THIS IS THE most critical area for dealing a deathblow to the Machiavellian Manager. Unfortunately, most organizations' performance appraisals, awards, and promotion systems promote the effectiveness of the Machiavellian Manager.

Personnel systems today, despite what the personnel experts assert, are not based on production and quality. Most personnel systems state that performance ratings and awards are to be based on guidelines the personnel experts themselves have contrived, and all employees are to be measured individually against these guidelines and associated standards as they apply to their positions. (Unfortunately, many unscrupulous personnel divisions today act as prostitutes for and receive favors from successful, powerful Machiavellian managers and executives.)

This is absurd. Everything else in life is relative; why shouldn't these systems be also? Under the personnel system in most organizations today, an employee with high-quality production can, and often does, receive a lower, if not much lower, rating than an average or mediocre producer. This distortion plays into the hand of the Machiavellian Manager, who does not—indeed, cannot under the personnel expert's rules—compare the productivity of one employee with that of another. Thus, the Machiavellian Manager can with impunity give very high ratings, numerous awards, and promotional opportunities to those who are loyal and nonthreatening to him.

Another result of this absurd personnel system is that some highly productive employees will, out of sheer frustration and desperation, resort to using Machiavellian Management strategies and techniques themselves since, to them, the organization is not really concerned

about high productivity and quality performance. At least they don't believe it is when
they observe countless organizational rewards
doled out to undeserving colleagues.

How can this counterproductive situation be
corrected? Here are several suggestions:

✗ Revamp the performance appraisal,
award, and, eventually, promotional systems to
reflect true productivity, timeliness, and quality
criteria by making the criteria associated with
these systems relative to the other employees'
productivity within the organization or unit.

✗ When employees win grievances against
their managers, make sure the managers pay the
consequences. Sanctions should be built into the
managers' performance appraisals. It is ridicu-
lous when managers lose even multiple grievances to employees, and bear no sanctions. Some
managers who have lost multiple grievances
have even won promotions, high performance
evaluations, and awards in organizations.

✗ Carefully review your subordinate manager's ratings of his employees. Compare the
ratings of each of his employees. If you are the
second-level supervisor of these employees, you
should have some idea as to whom the workers
are and the quality of their work. You should
also be aware if any of the employees have had
commendations from other units. A productive

worker with a relatively lower rating than those of mediocre employees should be a red flag to you.

✗ Have a genuine open-door policy for the nonsupervisory employees in your organization. It is essential that you occasionally communicate with these employees about their work. One way to effect this policy is to have a monthly informal lunch meeting with them, either with all of them at once or with designated groups. Such policies will greatly assist you in determining which ones are the most productive as well as whether your subordinate manager has real employee morale problems.

✗ Test your subordinate manager's performance by his answers to the following questions: Can he report verbally to you on organizational productivity measures and other organizational priorities without having to bring a subordinate staff member to the meeting?

Can he relate to you the number and kind of projects each of his employees is working on?

Does he have the ability to produce a quality product or report on his own without any assistance from his staff? (Give him an assignment and make it clear that he is to do it on his own.)

Does he take all the credit for good work produced in his unit without recognizing and crediting the employees who did the work?

Does he consistently state or imply that the quality work of an employee would never have been achieved without his intervention?

Does he engage in character assassination, especially of hard-working, highly productive employees?

✗ If you're really gutsy, establish a formal system whereby employees rate their supervisors. Throw out the best and the worst and let the accumulated employee ratings have a specified percentage effect or weight in your rating of your subordinate supervisor.

✗ Ensure that cost-saving proposals submitted to you by subordinate managers are not solely at the expense of employees without any commensurate sacrifice by the managers. Draconian cost-cutting measures can bring about short-term profits but can incur greater long-term costs because of lowered employee morale and exposure of such Draconian methods to the public and to potential job applicants, not to mention the media and stockholders.

✗ Establish an equitable method of recognizing the contributions of all managers and employees outside the organizational unit who are responsible for a major project. Often these external parties are recognized by organizations, but such recognition is most likely to be granted in cases where the parties are members of a powerful unit connected with the organization, even if their contributions have been minimal. Conversely, managers and employees of non-powerful organizational entities are often bled dry for their support and rarely receive any recognition. In other words, rewards go to those who count and not necessarily to those who have worked the hardest.

To ensure that credit is given where due, to enhance a sense of fairness, and to motivate employees throughout your organization, consider posting a notice similar to the following:

> Certain employees in Organization X, which is responsible for Project Y, are being considered for recognition for their outstanding efforts and contributions to our company. If you believe you have made an important contribution to this project and have not been informed by Organization X that you will be recognized, or if you believe the pending organizational recognition is unjustifiable, please notify Mr. Z in the Main Office. In keeping with our policy of fairness to all employees, your claim will be investigated and you will be informed of our decision.

✗ One area of performance that should be closely monitored by top-level executives is communication between divisions, or major components, of the organization. Too often vital communications between branches of a company go unanswered or are ignored. And if a response is forthcoming, it may be inappropriate to the issue raised.

This happens most frequently in two situations: (1) where one power unit is attempting to communicate with a competing power unit in circumstances where one party believes the other is a threat to its organizational preeminence; and (2) where a less-than-powerful organizational unit attempts to communicate a need to a higher-powered organizational component.

In both cases, the response or lack of same is dictated by organizational politics rather than by the mission at hand. If such communications breakdowns persist, the results can be disastrous for the entire organization.

To rectify, consider requiring that courtesy copies of *all* important correspondence between organizational divisions or components be sent to a top-level executive. Monitoring communications in this manner will go far in preventing internal struggles from interfering with the overall mission of the organization, especially if the results of such monitoring become part of the evaluation process for managers.

✗ Ensure that your subordinate managers report any project or programmatic problems to you. Most executives require such reports, but fail to make clear to their subordinate managers that they will be held accountable for any inaccurately reported problems or for not reporting problems that should have been reported or reported earlier. (This kind of information might finally be made available to you through an audit.) It is also important that this accountability be reflected in their performance appraisals.

✗ When a higher-level employee and a subordinate employee are making acrimonious charges against each other, do not automatically assume that the higher-level employee is right. Consider the employee history and integrity of both—techniques that are referred to in this book. If both are indeed organizationally productive and possess high integrity, simply tell them that you consider the charges and counter-charges unprofessional and unbecoming to both of them, and that the two should shake hands and work it out themselves.

✗ If you are authorized to take Draconian measures against an employee for abusing benefits or privileges, do not automatically agree to enforce such sanctions. A letter of reprimand will surely be sufficient while you instigate an internal audit to determine whether other employees are guilty of the same infringements. If others are not guilty, you may then issue a more severe disciplinary action against the guilty employee.

✗ If you haven't been giving only lip service to the modern-day motivational theories that insist that most employees are genuinely interested in increased productivity, profitability, increased service, and a quality work environment, then prove it. Let the employees select their colleagues for supervisory positions and let managers select their colleagues for executive positions. This will also help work against selecting an employee who is only too willing to forget where he or she came from. The only time this revolutionary concept would not be appropriate is when employees have been guilty of infringements requiring disciplinary or adverse action.

✗ Do not give bonuses to executives in companies when company profits have diminished or in government when cost-benefit ratios have declined. In Japan managers in similar positions would probably rather commit hara-kiri than accept such awards. Don't our organizational executives have any personal honor?

✗ Provide more group awards than individual rewards. Group awards encourage teamwork and an unselfish willingness to share talent and expertise. They also promote the philosophy that an organization is greater than any individual part, that is, one plus one equals five, not two. Group awards should be given not only to the highest performing organizational units, but also to those units that have had the highest increases in productivity.

The most important level for this kind of recognition is the first-level supervisory position and the supervisor's employees. The general rule in most organizations is that the higher the manager, the more frequent the awards and the higher value of those awards, often thousands of dollars. By contrast, the employees who made these awards possible receive, if lucky, a plaque, a pen and pencil set, or an "attaboy" memorandum.

Given all the status, power, prestige, salary, and benefits that higher-level managers receive, they should be the last in the organization to receive organizational awards for special efforts. High-level managers are paid for special efforts, and if they don't produce them, they should be removed.

✗. Eliminate unfair staffing practices. Alas, many high-level positions, especially positions like special assistants to high-level executives, are often filled otherwise than by full and open competition. Organizational personnel offices refer to these personnel actions as "alternate staffing methods" or "management needs actions." They even have the audacity to plead these staffing techniques as excuses for not selecting applicants who applied for these positions on the assumption that they were legitimate, open, and fully competitive opportunities.

Another closely associated technique is to fill a position by transfer, whereby the employee only laterals into another position. Then, after a decent interval, the manager promotes that employee based on the rationale that the job has "increased its level of classification criteria based on recent demands." Such personnel actions are nothing more than pure, unadulterated horsehockey.

Machiavellian Managers take full advantage of such systemic flaws to promote their loyal, unqualified lap dogs to these high-level positions. Therefore, by eliminating that sort of manipulation of staffing practices you will reduce the influence of Machiavellian Managers within your organization.

✄ Another way you can show faith in your colleagues is by trying to influence the selection of truly qualified individuals who came up through the ranks of the organization, to the board of directors. If you really have faith in the work force and are willing to prove it, try influencing a representative of the organization's union who is a nonsupervisory employee also to get elected. This sounds revolutionary, but unless our companies are ready to take revolutionary measures, they will not reclaim world leadership in their areas of enterprise.

It is imperative that nonsupervisory employees and their unions, supervisors, middle managers, executives, boards of directors, and stockholders all act as a team for the good of the organization if we are going to survive, if not excel, in the new world of international competition. If an organization cannot itself act as a team, how can it expect Uncle Sam to join in the organization's team efforts, as other national governments do for their businesses? Simply putting all the blame for our own lack of success on the Japanese or on the European Economic Community is a copout. It is not the traditional American way.

✗ Recognize the important contributions of every employee in the organization through equitable sharing in the organization's profits. How often in management courses do we impress upon our first-level supervisors their need to tell their employees how important they are to the success or failure of the organization? How often is that thinking expressed by top-level executives to the nonsupervisory employees in our organizations? These speeches are often politely referred to as pep talks by employees. In private they call them the "big organizational lie."

Why? The main reason is that the salary difference between nonsupervisory and management employees, especially in the United States, is enormous. When management tells its employees that "we all have to pull together for the good of the organization," nonsupervisory employees realize that the benefits of this effort will be distributed about 90 percent to management and 10 percent to them.

Organizations must either cut high-level management and executive salaries, or increase the salaries of its nonsupervisory work force, or both. We take great pride in being one of the greatest democratic societies in world history. Unfortunately, many of our organizations simply do not measure up to this claim.

✗ Establish an Employees Appreciation Month, similar to that of the United Fund Campaign. For contributions, target those whose salaries and benefits are in the upper 25 percent of the organization, but don't exclude employees at any level from contributing. As from time immemorial, many employees, even at the lowest levels, will donate a greater percentage of their salaries in appreciation for their jobs than will even a CEO or top-level senior executive service employee.

Like the United Fund Campaign, establish a goal and report on your organization's success in reaching the goal. One word of caution. Do not publish the names of those who give, and especially not the amounts. That information is between the employee and his conscience, or God. To publish such information cheapens the gift of the individual and substitutes organizational recognition for the rewards God gives each of us for such unselfishness.

After the donations have been received, distribute them equally among the lower 25 or 10 percent of wage earners in the organization in the form of a one-time check, presented privately. This might not amount to a lot for each person, but, to use an old cliché, the thought will surely count.

12

ESCAPING: TRANSFERRING OUT AND AWAY OR FINDING ANOTHER JOB

Without doubt princes become great when they overcome difficulties and opposition. . . .

IF YOU ARE a nonsupervisory employee or a low-level manager and do not have your own power base, or if your Machiavellian Manager is too well entrenched, your best option might be to transfer to another position within the organization or find another job outside the organization. That option may be the least traumatic for you.

One thing works to your advantage: your Machiavellian Manager doesn't want you around either. He wants only loyal lap dogs on his staff.

Provided you do not transfer to a position within the organization which he believes could be threatening to him, he will usually not stand in your way, and may even be cooperative.

✗ Evaluate your own knowledge, skills, and abilities, and determine if other units within the organization can use them. Check the X-118 Manual if you're in government service or your organization's eligibility criteria for other jobs within the organization. You need not transfer to an identical position. Many positions within an organization will qualify you for other kinds of positions that utilize all or part of your assets. Don't forget to include your past job experiences as well as off-the-job ones. These can be used to fill in the gaps, if needed.

✗ Identify friends in high places in the organization. They may hire you or help you get hired elsewhere in the organization.

✗ Consider weak power units within the organization. Competition for jobs there is usually not as keen as it is for positions in a strong unit. Management of a weak power unit may even be pleased that you are seeking a position there.

✗ Identify within your organization or another organization any unit that has just landed a big contract or a large budget increase. In this case, contemplate employment in a strong power unit.

✗ Ask your Machiavellian Manager if he would give up your position to another organizational unit. If you tell him you have a job prospect in a relatively weak power unit, he might be inclined to cede the position to get rid of you, even though it diminishes his empire slightly. He might also be concerned that if you don't leave, you might eventually file an official grievance.

✗ Act! Many employees who are victims of a Machiavellian Manager are in a quasi-state of shock. Such often produces inertia and a reluctance to place oneself further at the mercy of others. It also saps one's energy. Many employees lose heart when they think about all the work involved to update their job applications.

Don't be disheartened. Simply do an update to your application form and attach it to the front of your application. You can, if you prefer, pay someone to retype your application incorporating your update. Finally, you can always go to a recruitment agency. The point here is that you are actively doing something to address your situation, not just sitting back and becoming more and more depressed.

✗ Although it is very hard on the ego, consider applying for a lower-level job or even taking a voluntary downgrade. If you choose the latter, it might persuade your Machiavellian Manager that he is indeed right, that you have finally "seen the light." Your voluntary action would, it is hoped, take the pressure off you, for instead of always looking for things you do wrong, he might start taking note of the things you do right as a result of your "conversion." His change in attitude might even enable you eventually to return to your previous level.

There is no getting around the fact that this voluntary action is a gamble that might not work and might even backfire. It would probably be safer to seek a lower-level job under another supervisor, or, even better, in another agency or unit, or in a competitor's company. Managers outside your organization hold no loyalty to the management team in your organization and the values it promotes. Of course, in taking a lower-level job you may lose a few thousand dollars, but are the headaches of your present job worth the extra money?

13

STABBING BACK: FILING AN OFFICIAL GRIEVANCE

He . . . brought the Carthaginians to great extremities, so that they were obliged to come to terms with him. . . .

IF YOU HAVE no luck transferring out or getting another job in another organization, or you have just received a bad performance appraisal you cannot live with, file an official grievance. This is the least tasteful option since it will cause tension for you, but, it will also create stress for your Machiavellian Manager.

Regardless of the unpleasantness and hard work of this approach, it is a hundred times better than sitting back and playing the helpless victim. Doing nothing can cause you more grievous psychological and physiological damage by far than taking action will. Activity directed toward the problem is, in itself, healthful for you. Be sure, however, that you follow sound procedures in your action.

✗ Document every abuse and supervisory foulup concerning your performance committed by your Machiavellian Manager from the start of the rating period. Document the abuses of both his behavior and his job responsibilities as they relate to you. Include as accurately as you can all dates, details of his behavior, the misuse and abuse of his authority, a description of the poor guidance and direction he provided, and your response concerning each incident. Include witnesses to these events, if possible.

✗ Organize your documents so that they prove a pattern of poor supervision. You can organize either chronologically or topically (for instance, poor guidance). If you employ the latter method, then arrange the topics chronologically.

Another approach is to commence your grievance report by identifying the most grievous issues and then to proceed to the less grievous ones if you organize your report according to topics.

Leave nothing out. In your report show how, concerning each issue, you tried always to be responsive and cooperative. Show no mercy, but use no inflammatory language—obscenities, or strong descriptive words like creep, cutthroat, backstabber, or sycophant. Keep it professional.

✗ Review thoroughly your organization's grievance procedures and get a copy of your supervisor's performance standards. If you don't understand something clearly, seek advice from a personnel specialist (usually located in an employee-relations or labor-management section in the personnel office). Most personnel specialists will be willing to assist you and may even be appreciative that you have asked for their assistance.

✗ If you have a union in your organization or an Equal Employment Opportunity section, by all means consult it. Both organizations will not only provide you with useful guidance, but also usually assign a representative to deal with your Machiavellian Manager. They will also try to resolve the problem informally and quickly. If they cannot, they will assist you in the formal grievance or EEO complaint process.

✗ Never overlook procedure. The supervisor is usually obligated to follow certain time frames or dates, for example, when interim and final evaluations are to be given. Before he can give you a bad evaluation, he is usually obligated to give you the necessary guidance and time to improve so that a bad final evaluation will become unnecessary.

If he tells you during the interim evaluation that he is dissatisfied with your work, but refuses to give you an interim rating at that time, or just fills out the interim evaluation form without giving you a rating as to unsatisfactory or minimally satisfactory performance, this is a copout by him. His report is insufficient, and the date of the interim cannot be cited as giving you sufficient time to improve your performance, since he didn't give you a rating.

✗ Be patient and don't lose your cool, be methodical, and be timely. (This does not mean you should be friendly with your Machiavellian Manager at this point.) Realize that the grievance procedure is lengthy and time-consuming—you write your grievance, your Machiavellian Manager replies, you reply to his reply, he replies to your reply, and so on. At every stage, make sure your replies are timely. Take each point he makes and provide your best defense as a counterthrust. Then take the offensive in response to each point he makes, ignoring any highly inflammatory words he may use in his arguments—it is to your advantage to appear more professional than he.

✗ Publicize your grievance. Machiavellian Managers hate bad publicity, and as long as your adversary believes no one will become aware of how shabbily he is treating you, or if he can isolate the exposure, he will have a free hand to treat you as he pleases. Tell your colleagues in your unit and friends elsewhere in the organization that you are filing a grievance, but don't overdo it and become a bore. Also inform your third-level supervisor. Chances are your Machiavellian Manager has already informed on you and persuaded his boss that you deserve a bad rating or disciplinary action.

Advise your third-level supervisor that if the organization cannot resolve this grievance to your satisfaction informally, you will send a copy of your grievance to, and visit, if possible, the head of the organization. If you're a government employee, let him know you plan to send a copy of your formal grievance to your congressman and your agency's congressional oversight committees to notify them of the kind of management operating in the agency. You can even threaten to go to the press.

Finally, inform the third-level manager that if you have to file an official grievance, you will work as hard at seeing that sanctions are placed on any level of management supporting your Machiavellian Manager as you are at trying to win the grievance.

14

COUNTERESPIONAGE: WATCHING OUT FOR SOCIAL CONTACTS

How often the judgments of men in important matters are erroneous.

THERE IS AN old saying that more deals are cut on the golf course than inside the organization. Be ever observant of your subordinates' and colleagues' social behavior.

One of the biggest drawbacks in organizations' abilities to combat the Machiavellian Manager is the egos of the their managers. They love the unfailing flattery Machiavellian employees bestow on them. The competent manager earns the respect of his employees, colleagues, and superiors through his concern about high employee morale, rewarding the deserving based on their productivity, being concerned about the organization's productivity, and providing good guidance and leadership. He demonstrates his capability of producing a quality product on his own through working hard. No manager can demand that his employees, colleagues, or superiors respect him.

Unfortunately, managers abound who are much more concerned that their employees idolize and patronize them by virtue of their position in the organization. They love being surrounded by admirers who thrill to their every word on any subject. They often remind one of a king or prince holding audience. Machiavellian Managers take the utmost advantage of these unprofessional, egomaniacal managers. Chances are, these managers are themselves Machiavellian Managers, albeit not clever ones. Here is how you can identify some of the types:

✄ Mark which managers constantly appear to be holding court and the toadies who make up their retinue. This is especially observable at off-site organizational conferences during after hours. The effective manager will also socialize, but at the same time will be seen trying to work out productivity problems and will not always be observed in the same company. Stable, well-balanced, and productive nonsupervisory employees will also associate and socialize not only with higher-level management on occasion, but also separately with their own peers.

✗ Notice if a subordinate employee or colleague starts showing up in religious and or social organizations you or your family belongs to. A few apt questions can help you determine whether his membership is a result of a "new interest" or reflects an interest he has been engaged in over time.

✗ Observe employees at training courses. Do they mingle with classmates or are they, when given the chance, interacting with the highest-level managers in the class? Do they appear interested more in this interaction than in attending to the course content? If an opportunity for kudos arises, do they flatter the high-level managers, even though their contributions to the class were minimal?

Finally, determine if any employees are not qualified technically, according to the course's admission criteria, for the training course. Carefully observe their behavior until you are confident they are genuinely interested in the course content and not in currying favor.

✗ Be cautious of employees who seek out you more frequently than other employees and direct the conversation to non-job-related subjects. Do you believe they really must know your opinion on all subjects in order to be productive employees? Be wary of flattery.

✗ Do the same employees always want to eat lunch with you? Do they come to your house to do yard work, help with your car repairs, or aid in construction projects around the house? If so, how can you be objective in evaluating them, especially if you are comparing their performances with those of your other employees? Such behavior will not only create the impression that you have favorites, but also make others sincerely doubt that you will apply the same performance standards to them as you do to your favorites. They thus will doubt that your evaluations are objective. That will breed serious motivational problems within your unit.

✗ Beware of those who habitually complain, and engage in character assassination, of others in the organization, especially of their own colleagues. Such employees are trying to elevate themselves by belittling the efforts and personalities of others. And bear in mind that it is but one easy step for these schemers to take before they start plunging the knife into you, especially if you do not treat them better than their colleagues.

✗ Do you have employees who eagerly flock to the presence of higher-level managers when they visit your unit, or of those managers at conferences? Such subordinates will often attempt to manipulate upper-level managers into believing that they have great admiration for them, much more even than you have for those superiors.

15

COUNTERINTELLIGENCE: REVIEWING AN EMPLOYEE'S ORGANIZATIONAL HISTORY

When you see the minister think more of himself than of you, . . . such a man will never be a good minister.

ACCORDING TO SANTAYANA, unless we are willing to learn from history, we are condemned to repeat it. Employees who have been or are currently victims of Machiavellian Managers are greatly baffled that upper-level management appears so oblivious to the antics of these managers, and, particularly baffled when the latter receive high performance appraisal ratings, awards, and promotional opportunities.

Managers are themselves often equally perplexed when someone they have selected and promoted will, of a sudden and without provocation, turn against them and ally with an organizational enemy or engage in backstabbing techniques.

There is no substitute for knowing an employee's past organizational history. Here are ways to guard against being defrauded:

X Never rely solely on an employee's application form or his personnel records. These documents will give you only the bare-bones employment history and boring administrative details. The one thing of value you can glean from them is help in determining how quickly the employee has been advanced, and where or whom to contact to identify his former colleagues.

X Contact at least two colleagues with whom the job applicant has worked and his past supervisors. Be careful. His previous peers might be unjustifiably jealous and his previous supervisors might themselves be Machiavellian Managers. On the other hand, they might also be victims of this employee's behavior. Look for patterns and a preponderance of evidence.

X If the employee applying for a promotion or job comes from your organization, you will more easily be able to determine if he is a Machiavellian Manager. Besides which, you should by now be able to discern Machiavellian managerial strategies and techniques, thereby enabling you to conclude whether the managers who promoted the employee are themselves Machiavellian Managers. They often breed other Machiavellian Managers.

✗ Check for any casualties among those who have worked with the one applying for a promotion or job. Have his colleagues or supervisors exhibited psychological and physiological stress symptoms? Have any of them been removed from their positions, transferred, or demoted? Has the applicant, as a supervisor, had high employee turnover on his staff? Answers to these questions should help you determine what sort of character you are dealing with.

✗ If the employee you are considering hiring or promoting is a supervisor, has he provided awards to his staff? If so, what kind of awards? Have more individual than group awards been given? Have any individual awards been of questionable merit? Have awards gone only to those who appear to be merely average producers but loyal lap dogs of the supervisor? The last two questions should also be applied to employees the supervisor promoted.

✗ Has the same supervisor provided for career training opportunities for his staff, and have these opportunities been provided for all his employees? Has the supervisor encouraged his employees to apply for higher-level positions within the organization? Has the supervisor ever displayed indignation over or complained about employee ingratitude when a worker transfers to another job, or gets selected for and promoted to another job?

✗ Beware of a supervisor who has lost an employee grievance. It would be in your best interest to check into the grounds of the grievance and why the supervisor failed to win the case. If the supervisor has lost several employee grievances, forget considering him.

16

RELYING ON YOUR INNER STRENGTHS AND SEEKING ASSISTANCE

Men act right only upon compulsion.

ARE YOU INTROSPECTIVE? Most of us question our motives and behaviors, consider where we are going in life, determine what our true values are, and ponder anew what is really important in our lives only when we are suffering considerable tension, anxiety, or depression. When everything seems fine, we're too busy or having too much fun for self-analysis.

Perhaps this sounds trite, but periods of strong emotions occasioned by prolonged stress may be part of life's way of testing us, and forcing us to grow in spite of our unwillingness to do so. These times erode our pride and enable us to tap into our own God-given inner strengths and to be willing to obtain help. Legions of people like you have done this, and been elated at the strength and courage they have received.

✗ Seek help from a certified psychologist or psychiatrist. There is no shame in doing this, and no one need know about it. All of us get out of balance more often than we care to admit. However, when we are having trouble getting ourselves back into balance, this can cause physiological and psychological damage.

What the psychologist and psychiatrist will do is provide professional assistance in helping you get back into balance. They will assist you both in arriving at an accurate, realistic description of your problem and in identifying and implementing your own solutions.

✗ Seek the guidance of your spiritual leader or others who are of your religious persuasion. Go one on one, or participate in group support meetings.

✗ Don't be afraid to consult your friends. That friend of yours who appears to be so successful and well balanced has, almost assuredly, gone through similar or other traumatic experiences of his own. You will be comforted in knowing that your own trauma is not unique or unusual, and may not be nearly as devastating as your friend's experiences were.

✗ If you are a spiritual person, pray and meditate frequently. Prayer is speaking to God or the universal source of intelligence or conscience; meditation is listening to the same. Most of us don't need much guidance on praying—"just do it," as the song says.

But many of us may be unfamiliar with meditation. Consult your local library. Much has been written on this subject. Transcendental Meditation is perhaps the best known of many techniques. If meditation appeals to you, you might entertain going on a retreat or taking a course in the subject.

✗ Don't isolate your job problems from your spouse or loved one. You may think you're protecting that one from unnecessary grief, or be too ashamed to admit to having job problems. Any love relationship requires honesty and cannot long survive without it. Our loved ones know when we are troubled, and they have the right to know what is distressing us. They will also support us. However, you need not overburden them with your problems; simply acknowledge that you have them and they will better understand your behavior.

If they volunteer help, accept it. It is up to you, however, whether or not to adopt their recommendations. That decision must be yours. Otherwise, if you apply a loved one's recommendation and it doesn't work, you may end up blaming that one for all your problems.

X If you have children, you must also inform them when you are having job difficulties. We all want to appear as successful, mature authority figures to our children. We guide them through their problems, and not vice versa, right? Your children, like all normal children, will experience in one form or another by the time they get to your age the same kind of job stress that you have faced. Perhaps the greatest legacy you can leave them with is not your brilliant career, but your courage in confronting adversity, admitting it, and eventually conquering it without having to sacrifice the love of your children.

X A prophet of recent times has stated that the best way to help oneself is to help others. When we suffer from considerable job stress and anxiety, that suffering tends to dominate our consciousness and affect our behavior every moment of the day. We isolate ourselves and become obsessed with ourselves.

Look around for ways to help others, either on the job or off the job, or both. Volunteer your services to civic, religious, or social organizations. If you doubt this will work a positive change in your life, I dare you to try it.

Remember, the world's great religions, in one way or another, state that good eventually overcomes evil, and that the pursuit of goodness (Godliness or being one with the universal conscience or intelligence) is the primary reason for our existence.

17

INCREASING ORGANIZATIONAL AWARENESS

A wise prince should . . . never remain idle in peaceful times, but industriously make good use of them, so that when fortune changes she may find him prepared to resist her blows, and to prevail in adversity.

NOT EVERYBODY WILL rush out to buy a copy of this handbook. But if you believe the behavior of the Machiavellian Manager can create dysfunction in an organization, and you would like to help ensure that his kind of behavior is avoided in your organization, then expose your staff to the concepts in this handbook. Sponsor or conduct a training course in your organization based on this volume.

One key to the success of the Machiavellian Manager is his subtlety. He never honestly reveals his strategies and techniques to his colleagues, employees, or supervisors. Exposure of his stratagems by increasing your staff's awareness of them will go a long way toward disarming him, and discouraging others to follow in his footsteps.

If it is too expensive for your organization to sponsor training courses based on this handbook, then you might wish to buy copies of it and make it required reading of your staff. To ensure they read it, you might ask each one to write a report on it and submit it to you.

It is not important to me that you and your organization agree with all of my recommendations on how to deal with the Machiavellian Manager. What is important to me, and I hope to you, is that this handbook will help to inspire a healthy reexamination and discussion of the quality of organizational life in our times. I also hope it will lead to the realization that dysfunctional organizational activities are caused first and foremost by individuals and not by computers or other so-called wonders of modern technology, or by the material work environment. Nor do such activities arise because your organization is located in icy, cold, rural International Falls, Minnesota, or in sunny, hot, metropolitan Miami.

It is also important to me that this book contribute to a greater recognition of and respect for individuals within an organization, regardless of the position they hold. Every person is entitled to his or her dignity and sense of self-worth, regardless of whether that person is a top-level executive or the lowest clerk-typist. Too often organizations give the impression that the value of an individual as a human being is directly related to the position that person occupies. When organizations promote that attitude, either intentionally or unintentionally, it is no wonder that some people in it will resort to the most destructive kinds of Machiavellian behavior.

I am not suggesting that managers have no right or obligation to perform their management functions and enforce discipline. But too often conversations between a manager and a subordinate are conducted in a tone of one superior human being talking down to a lesser species. All of us must ever remember that we are subordinate employees regardless of our positions in an organization. In government the president's cabinet is answerable to the president and Congress, and they in turn are answerable to the people. In a corporation the president or CEO is answerable to his stockholders. If you are ever concerned about how your boss is treating you, ask yourself first how you have been treating employees below you. You can control your own behavior, but can only hope at best to influence that of others. The best way to do that is by example.

High-level managers and executives must be ready to relinquish power and abandon elitism for a representative, popular mandate from the employees of the organization. They must forgo their enormous salaries, awards, and bonuses made possible by organizations; in place of them they must be prepared to accept the gratitude, respect, and honor that employees and their families will readily bestow on them for their willingness to share their authority and wealth with the workers.

The United States, as perhaps the world leader in influencing the affairs of mankind, must either apply the principles of the world's great religions in its organizations, or surely lose its spiritual mandate and historic opportunity provided and made possible by God. If this challenge is not successfully met, another nation or nations will surely arise and be handed this torch.

Here a little, there a little, one step at a time. If we cannot bring about improvements in the organizations where we work, have we the right to expect our representatives in Congress and the White House to enact the changes demanded by our consciences and what we intrinsically know to be God's will? In particular we should remember the Golden Rule (Matthew 7:12): "Do unto others as you would have others do unto you."

Whether or not you decide to take action based on this book is up to you, of course. Allow me only a final admonition: Although I have slightly exaggerated parts of the descriptions of Machiavellian Managers, the beasts are out there. If you don't believe me, just look around—or in a mirror.

APPENDIX:
NICCOLÒ MACHIAVELLI

NICCOLÒ MACHIAVELLI (1469–1527) was a Florentine bureaucrat and diplomat during a turbulent time in Italian history. He served the republican government of his city with distinction, observing firsthand the powerbrokers both in Florence and in foreign cities where he performed diplomatic functions for his government. He was reputed to be an excellent administrator and organizer, and held positions equivalent to a modern chief magistrate's chief of staff or cabinet secretary.

When the dictatorial Medici family was restored to power in Florence in 1512, Machiavelli was exiled from the city and deprived of the livelihood at which he excelled and which for him was the essence of life itself. He was unable to get himself restored to favor by the Medicis and spent the remainder of his life in political isolation writing the works that have made him famous. The best known but by no means most important of them is *The Prince*.

The term *Machiavellian* suggests to us something evil in nature. We associate the term with leaders like Napoleon, Mussolini, and Hitler. But Machiavelli himself would not have approved of many or even most of the actions of those leaders, but merely have observed that their success derived from the employment of certain techniques in their exercise of power, techniques which he most eloquently set forth in *The Prince*.

Machiavelli almost defies labeling in today's political vernacular. He can be called with some justification a liberal in that he supported the republican government of Florence, and a humanist in that he separated the theory of the exercise of power from theological or ethical considerations. But whatever other label we might like to pin on Machiavelli, he was above all else a realist. He saw what worked among the powerbrokers of early fifteenth-century southern Europe and recorded it. Given the instability of Italian politics and the chaos that resulted from the shifting of power from one locus to another, Machiavelli did, quite reasonably, advocate stability. It seems safe to conclude from what we know of him that he would have willingly sacrificed a certain amount of individual freedom for a degree of harmony within the state. He seemed to recognize that people can be harmed as much by political upheaval as by the deliberate if not ruthless exercise of power by those in positions of authority. In that context he can be called a conservative.

Machiavelli's work has also been styled radical or revolutionary for he broke with traditional attitudes and philosophies about political power. As a political historian he understood the principal uses of power within the Roman Republic and Empire and was probably familiar with the histories of the Greek city-states. He understood that the uses of power had evolved over time and wished to contribute to that evolutionary process.

Whatever Machiavelli was, or whatever he believed, he is very much alive today, as a fascinating specimen of medieval bureaucrat, a political philosopher, and a patron of many who both understand, and fail miserably to grasp, what he was about.